Ina's Way

A story of courage and love

Sarah Swedler and Elaine Medline

Books that inspire, help and heal

Creative Bound Inc.
Box 424, Carp, Ontario K0A 1L0
(613) 831-3641

Published by Creative Bound Inc. on behalf
of the Swedler family. Net proceeds to the Ina Swedler McCarthy
Memorial Fund at the Juvenile Diabetes Foundation (Canada).

ISBN 0-921165-64-1
Printed and bound in Canada

Written by Sarah Swedler and Elaine Medline
Cover art by Harley Swedler
Book design by Wendelina O'Keefe

Canadian Cataloguing in Publication Data

Swedler, Sarah
    Ina's way : a story of courage and love

ISBN 0-921165-64-1

    1. McCarthy, Ina Swedler, 1966-1996 2. Diabetes in
children—Patients—Canada—Biography. 3. Diabetics—
Canada—Biography. I. Medline, Elaine, 1964- II. Title.

RJ420.D5S94 1999   362.1'9892462'0092   C99-900868-4

To
Joshua

— ◇ —

Acknowledgments

Thank you, my husband Arnie, for all your love and support, and for helping each day with our grief, bringing us closer together. No matter what, your children and I always came first. I need your love now more than ever. Thank you for allowing me to do things the Sarah way.

Thanks to Harley and Jane, Jared, Marlee and Andi for making life worth living.

And to my nieces and nephews—my love for you will always be there. To my sister Nettie and my brother-in-law Harry, my brother Sam and my sister-in-law Edna. Without your constant support, I could not have made it. Also remembering my sister Anne, the matriarch of the family who was loved by all.

To Rabbi Bulka for your spiritual guidance. It was you who coined the phrase, "Ina's Way."

To all my closest and dearest friends, who have felt my pain and pulled me out of the house, and who understand when I don't want to go.

To my loving cousins, who have been by my side.

To Dr. Bill James, friend and physician.

To Dr. David Waiser, who has helped me.

To Dr. Margaret Lawson, Dr. David Levine, Dr. Erin Keeley, Dr. Piney Pollock, Dr. Max della Zazzera and the dialysis teaching unit at the Ottawa General Hospital, especially Cheryl.

To the Kidney Foundation of Ottawa.

To the Ladies of the Nine Hole League, who keep in touch even in the winter from Florida.

To Elaine Medline, for being a pleasure to work with. I wish her much success in her future endeavors.

To the staff of the *Ottawa Citizen*, *Ottawa Sun*, and *Ottawa Business Journal*. Special thanks to Mark Sutcliffe for always being there, and for your beautiful tribute to Ina in your newspaper.

Thanks to the Ottawa community, particularly Ina's colleagues and friends and all those who are helping to keep Ina's memory alive. And a special thanks to all of Ina's friends who are always there for Josh.

Introduction

After the loss of my beloved daughter Ina, my best friend, I collected newspaper articles that included such wonderful comments about this exceptional woman. Then, as weeks went on, I started looking through old photos and articles that Ina had written, and I placed them in a scrapbook. I decided to fill this scrapbook with mementoes of Ina's life, from the first minute of her life until her death. I found her hospital bracelet, her report cards, the notes she wrote in hospital, etc., and as I taped them all in the book I couldn't see through my tears. I remembered all the wonderful times, the parties we had, the laughter, and slowly, I made a vow to always keep Ina's memory alive.

This book, *Ina's Way*, was written for Josh, so that he will understand what a special person his mother was. I want him to know how much she adored him.

I think that many mothers and daughters who read this book will be able to relate to the relationship Ina and I shared. I also hope the book will help people who are struggling with their illnesses.

My pain is with me 24 hours a day and it will never go away. I'm an actress. I go out and people say, "you look good." But there's not a moment I don't feel the pain. There is no such thing as 'time heals.' That isn't what you want to hear. You want to hear, 'You're my friend and I accept you for who you are.' You never get over the loss of a child.

But then I think of the positive things. I think of all the time I spent with Ina. I think of how I allowed her to live her life her way. She traveled all over the world, went to university out of town, had lots of friends and got married. Her greatest achievement was having Josh. I feel both happiness and sadness when I see Josh. He's a bright boy, so bubbly. There is so much of Ina in him. It is so wonderful to be with him. But I feel sad that Ina cannot see him. She would be so proud.

Sarah Swedler, 1999

CHAPTER 1

Cartwheeling Her Problems Away

Ina cartwheeled down the hospital hallway, several times a day, every day for ten days. She spun over the cold tiles, past the doctors and nurses and orderlies, who must have smiled when they saw her. This was Ina's way, to dance amidst adversity, to keep her life moving, to remain calm while others worried for her. She was 10 years old. She had just been diagnosed with diabetes. It was June, 1976.

A young gymnast, Ina trained three hours a night at Ottawa's Corona Gym Club. She was healthy, as far as anyone could tell. A bit thin, but that came from exercising so much. She was a sweet kid, a Nancy Drew fan, a tree-climber, a lover of bubblegum—the kind that comes with comics wrapped inside. She wore long pigtails. Her father Arnie owned a food distribution company—Arnie's Food Services, The Fresh Guys—specializing in chickens. Her mother Sarah had just opened a women's clothing store with a friend. Her brother Harley, who was four years older, adored his giddy little sister, even if he did sometimes call her Goody-Two-Shoes.

They lived in a grey-brick bungalow with a circular driveway. Their house, on Linton Road in the south end of Ottawa, was located in a new suburb where children filled the streets and all the moms knew each other. Ina brought home the finest report cards. Boys were crazy about her. A young admirer once sat at the end of her driveway for hours one day with his dog, only waiting for Ina to come home. Every Sunday night, the Swedlers would meet the Zunder family for supper at the Kardish deli. Ina liked her dad to tickle her feet. It was a good childhood.

And the summer of 1976 was going to be a special one for Ina. For the first time, she would spend a month at sleepover camp, Camp B'nai B'rith on the Ottawa River. It was a Jewish summer camp about 45 minutes from the city. To attend, a routine medical exam was mandatory. That's when diabetes first appeared, during that routine test. It was such an innocent medical exam, more of an annoyance than anything else. Three days after that routine exam, the pediatrician—a friend of the family—phoned to say there seemed to be a problem with Ina's urine. He was sure it was a mistake. The urine sample happened to be sitting beside a bottle of cleaning fluid, and likely got contaminated.

There were no symptoms of diabetes. Ina wasn't overly thirsty. She wasn't overly tired. Someone who was sick wouldn't be able to do backflips off a beam, would they? The doctor asked Sarah to bring in another urine sample whenever she got a chance. There was no panic. This was a peppy kid, after all. The test was repeated, and the doctor immediately admitted Ina to the Children's Hospital of Eastern Ontario for further testing. The hospital confirmed diabetes. And as Ina did cartwheels down the hallway, her mother Sarah sat on a concrete step outside the building and sobbed.

So began Ina's life of diabetes, of insulin injections and testing and sugarless food. For her, diabetes was a nuisance, a bother, a waste of time. In truth, diabetes got in Ina's way. For her, life as a diabetic was a life of yearning—yearning to be normal, yearning to be spontaneous, and yearning, most of all, to be cured.

Diabetes is a life regulated by blood sugar levels, a life unimaginable to anyone who has never experienced it. There are two types of diabetes, type 1 and type 2. Type 2 diabetes occurs in adults and can be controlled by exercise, weight loss and medications. In type 1, or juvenile diabetes, the insulin-making cells of the pancreas become faulty and make little or no insulin. In Canada, 10 to 15 out of every 100,000 people will get type 1 diabetes each year. Insulin controls blood sugar levels, and without it a person will sink into a coma and die. That's why type 1 diabetics give themselves insulin injections, and why they test their blood sugar regularly. It's a way to manage the disease. It's not a cure. Generally, as life goes on, complications arise, one by one—complications like kidney disease and heart problems, infections and blindness and amputations. Life expectancy is lower for diabetics. Nowadays, researchers are trying to curb the complications. There's better sugar control, surgery to prevent blindness, more valiant attempts to handle the high blood pressure that leads to kidney problems. Still, it's not an easy disease. It was never easy, even after insulin was discovered in 1922.

"Every time that needle went into her, it stabbed my heart," Sarah says, "Every time that needle went into her."

After that first visit to the Children's Hospital, Sarah wasted no time learning about the disease that had taken hold of Ina. Sarah was, of course, aware of diabetes. In fact, her neighbor's two-year-old daughter had been diagnosed with it before Ina, and she knew never to give the girl candy. (Why is she making such a fuss, the women on the street said about that mother. "No one knew the hardship she had to go through," Sarah says now.) Sarah knew almost nothing about the disease. She looked up the number of the Canadian Diabetes Association in the phone book, and couldn't find it there. In those days, the Children's Hospital of Eastern Ontario had no organized program to initiate the new diabetic. So Sarah began reading. She forced herself to learn the facts, to see what was in store for her only daughter. Sarah learned everything she could about diabetes. She learned, and she worried. Perhaps she learned too much. When she heard about dialysis—the treatment for failed kidneys, including failed kidneys of diabetics—she began avoiding the dialysis room at the hospital. Even if it meant going out of her way a bit, even if it meant taking extra stairs, she would avoid passing this room. And when she did have to pass this room, she cringed. To her, dialysis represented a bleak future for

Ina. Sarah knew everything diabetes could do, and slowly, what she feared came true.

Eventually, Ina would need dialysis, and it stabbed Sarah's heart.

Diabetes brought Sarah and Ina closer together, and diabetes drove them apart. When they fought, it was because of diabetes. Ina often said she herself didn't have to worry, because her mother worried for her. Sarah knew her every move and worried every minute. All these years later, one sentence in one of those books read by Sarah in the early days stands out for her. "When a child is diabetic, there are two patients," the book said. "One is the child, and the other is the mother."

Ina wasn't famous, and Sarah didn't discover some miracle cure. That's how it might happen in the movies, but that's not how it goes in life, usually. Ina would have liked to become famous; she had dreams of being a TV talk show host. And Sarah did help raise many thousands of dollars for the diabetes cause, in hopes of a cure. Both women wanted to live life in a big way. They were alike in that way.

This book is a celebration of a brave daughter's life, from the perspective of a mother. It's about a mother and daughter struggling against an illness, not always in step, but always together. It's about a mother trying to keep her daughter's memory and dreams alive, about a mother trying to overcome her own devastation. There is a bit of Ina in every daughter, and a bit of Sarah in all mothers. What mother isn't concerned about her daughter? And what daughter doesn't want to go her own way?

Yet Sarah and Ina's relationship was also unique, because Sarah was so tenacious, and Ina so sick, and both of them always so scared and so hopeful.

On Sarah's kitchen table is a scrapbook of memories. On the cover is a picture of Ina as an adult, a journalist sitting in front of her computer. Beneath the adult picture is Ina's hospital bracelet at birth, her birth certificate, and a blurry photograph of her in her hospital crib. She was a small baby, weighing five pounds, fourteen ounces.

Sarah was the sort of mother who kept everything. The scrapbook contains so many kept memories. There's a cute letter, for example, for Sarah on Mother's Day, which Ina wrote when she was eight.

> *Dear Mom,*
>   *I love you so much because you are so nice to me. I've said so many bad things to you I hope you forgive me. I hope on this Mother's Day you have a very nice one. And I will try to please you if you do not make me ware [sic] those white shirts that I hate. You work so hard for me and Harley. You by us close [sic], make our beds wash the dishes and so many other things.*

The scrapbook also includes old birthday cards, and a typewritten note from Ina's primary school, advising Sarah and Arnie that she would skip a grade. There's a funny account by Ina of her years at McGill University; it's called "The Undergraduates." Ina also wrote an article for the *Ottawa Citizen* about the Jewish New Year, Rosh Hoshanah, accompanied by a picture of Sarah and Ina in the kitchen cutting dough for potato knishes. The article helped Ina land her husband Stuart. Part of it went like this:

"My mother Sarah spends hours preparing for the traditional Rosh Hoshanah meal," Ina wrote. "No matter how many people are invited for the meal, there is always double the amount of food, 'just in case.' Like most Jewish mothers, my mom's motto is 'no one should be alone on the Jewish Holidays.' When my brother Harley was an architecture student he always invited at least five hungry friends for the meal if they could not travel home to spend the holiday. One student came to our house three years in a row, until he finally asked Harley why he was always invited. Harley repeated my mother's feelings, and his friend responded with a surprising answer. "Harley, I hate to tell you this, but I'm not even Jewish."

Also in the scrapbook is a letter that Sarah wrote to Ina the day Ina left for a summer in Israel at age 19.

Well, it's finally arrived. The day you have so long waited for...Ina, I know it has not been easy for you and sometimes I have nagged, cried, yelled and did not speak to you. I realize now and I think you do know that we only want what's best for you. I will miss you more than words can describe. You are my best friend who understands exactly the way I feel. When I have to say something that's on my mind who

13

but you can I tell. When I don't finish a sentence you know what I mean. We laugh together and cry together. The important thing is you are always there. I am going to miss you so much but will be happy knowing you are having a ball. LECTURE TIME. 1. Please take good care of yourself. 2. When in doubt what to eat, what you think might make you sick, don't eat it. 3. Drink loads of water and diet drinks. 4. Please don't get burned from the sun, use lots of suntan oil. 5. Wear a hat when you are working in the fields. 6. If you don't feel well, don't think it might be this or that, see a Doctor—let him tell you. 7. Don't get overtired. I could go on but I know you are smart enough to take care. We love you so much so please come back to us well. Enjoy and shalom.

    Love you,
    Mom and Dad

Sarah has just turned 60, although she looks much younger, pretty, blond and stylish. She does nautilus twice a week, plays golf when she can, and more than ever, raises money for diabetes research. She has given up her volunteer job as president of the auxiliary at Hillel Lodge, a home for seniors in Ottawa, but still visits the residents, taking them out to nice restaurants for lunch. She has four grandchildren, Jared, Marlee, Andi and Josh. Josh is the son of Ina and Stuart.

Sarah and Arnie moved out of the house on Linton Road a few years back and now live in a condominium on the Ottawa canal, where they can watch the tour boats cruise along in the summer and the skaters speed by in the winter. Life is hard for Sarah now. Condolence letters fill half her scrapbook.

Sarah sometimes climbs the stairs to the guest room, opens the cupboard, and touches the white terry cloth bathrobe that's hanging there. Tears fill her eyes. The bathrobe appears so clean, so soft, so delicate with its lacy sleeves. The bathrobe was originally Sarah's. It was given to Ina when Ina was staying at the Toronto Hospital in the fall of 1996. During that hospitalization, Sarah noticed her daughter shivering as she struggled to walk along the hospital corridor. The white terry cloth bathrobe was still Sarah's then. Sarah had brought it to Toronto for herself, as she was staying in a hotel near the hospital. Sarah held Ina's arm as they walked together down the hallway, remembering how her little girl once tumbled along the hospital corridor. She wanted Ina to have her bathrobe.

"I'll bring it to you, Ina," Sarah said. "You're shivering."

CHAPTER 2

Ina's Way

Harley can still hear Ina laugh. Her laugh had an incredible giddiness, as if she couldn't quite believe what was happening around her. Her eyebrows would pop up, her chin would drop, and the laughter would begin. It was a rolling laugh, continual, she couldn't stop. You knew when Ina was in the room even when you couldn't see her, because of her laugh.

When Harley and Ina were young, Sarah and Arnie took them to a fancy restaurant in Hull, across the river from Ottawa. The maître d' pulled out Ina's chair, but Ina didn't realize it, and she fell on the floor, bursting into laughter. Then, when the maître d' lit Sarah's cigarette for her, the laughter began again. There was so much laughter. Ina laughed because Sarah—known to murder the English language—never seemed to make much sense and often called people by their wrong names. ("Mom, it's sad," Ina would say. "I'm beginning to understand you.") Just before Ina's marriage to Stuart, Sarah was so nervous she called a woman Ignorant whose name was really Ingrid. Ina laughed when Sarah's honeycake was a flop four times in a row. Ina laughed at her father too, because his business practices were so old-fashioned he kept the cash in a cigar box, and she wasn't above laughing at herself, at her own hugely swollen legs that came with being pregnant with Josh.

Sarah used to say to her children: "Too much laughter brings crying."

It's a saying Harley repeats to his three children, and Sarah once heard Ina tell it to Josh, whose laugh sounds just like Ina's.

The Swedler family's laughter did eventually turn to tears. Sarah now believes Ina knew she wouldn't live long, so she wanted to live her life in her own way.

"She was almost out to prove that this was not a disease that was going to get her down. As a parent to stand by this...," Sarah says, trailing off.

The first argument was over camp. Ina was scheduled to go to B'nai B'rith just a few weeks after she was diagnosed with diabetes. There was also a camp for children with diabetes nearby, a place that was safe for children with the disease, where children could learn about taking care of themselves, where they could meet other kids with the same problems. Any parent would feel better knowing their child was attending such a camp. But Ina refused to attend the diabetic camp. She longed to go to B'nai B'rith, even though she didn't know anyone else who was going there too. Ina didn't want to be a person with diabetes, and was so insistent on the camp question that Sarah gave in quickly. Sarah's late sister Annie couldn't believe Sarah would send her daughter to a regular camp so soon after she was diagnosed. Annie didn't talk to Sarah for three weeks because of it.

That first summer at camp was hard for Ina, at first. Dutifully she walked to the infirmary every morning to give herself her insulin injection. But diabetes wasn't what gave her problems. Ina was lonely. She phoned her parents one day, asking to return home. The camp doctor assured Arnie and Sarah that Ina was healthy, just homesick, and had been crying for hours. Arnie wanted to pick up Ina immediately, but Sarah said no. Don't get excited, Sarah told Arnie. All children get lonely at camp.

"Sure enough, she ended up loving it. Where I got the strength to send her to camp! My husband was so furious with me. Everybody was screaming at me, my family especially. Can you believe I did that?" Sarah asks now, confounded by her former fortitude.

The friends Ina made at B'nai B'rith were friends for life. Lori Chazonoff, Donna Hart, Leslie Greenberg to name a few. Ina came home with awards etched in wood, Miss Congeniality and Most Popular. Her favorite activity was tennis. Jokingly, Ina berated her mother for enrolling her in gymnastics instead of tennis. She said she could have been a tennis star. Normally humble, Ina did have one personality quirk—she badly wanted fame.

Eventually, Ina became the dance instructor at B'nai B'rith. On special occasions, such as when the camp put on the musical *Tommy*, Sarah and Arnie drove up with parcels of smoked meat and deli sandwiches.

Most teenagers with diabetes rebel in some way. Those teenage years are difficult for anyone. But to be a teenager and diabetic, the challenges are huge. A diabetic life is so regulated, so abnormal, so time-consuming. Bad eating habits, skipping insulin shots, lying about testing—one-third of teens with diabetes do it. After a year of living with the disease, Ina started slipping. She liked to binge. She gobbled down tubs of ice cream and M & Ms, whipped cream cookies and Hershey Kisses. She didn't always test. She didn't keep her log regularly, and Sarah suspects she lied when she did. She played with her insulin, giving herself a half-dose now and then, in order to lose weight— a common strategy among teenage girls with diabetes. For Ina, high blood sugar was a bigger problem than low blood sugar. With low blood sugar, diabetics get dizzy and may pass out. However, with high sugar—usually a sign of poor control—people go into what's called diabetic ketoacidosis. The sugar can't get into cells, and this brings about such an extreme chemical imbalance in the body that severe vomiting, dehydration and hospitalization can result. It's life-threatening. On average, this happened to Ina several times a year.

Ina also suffered infection after infection, as the immune cells don't work well when the blood sugar level is off. When Ina had a cold, it's wasn't just a cold; she sometimes ended up in hospital. When she cut herself, she could end up in a doctor's office getting the cut lanced and cleaned and dressed. She had abscesses on her head and styes in her eyes. One year she was in and out of hospital seven times. Ina's friend Arlie Koyman recalls visiting Ina in hospital, watching Ina suck water from the damp cloth on her forehead, thirsty yet forbidden to take a glass of water while on intravenous fluid.

Although she did argue with her mother at times and was often terribly sick, Ina was known in the community as a kind and bubbly girl, a loyal friend with a wonderful sense of humour.

"She was an incredible person," says her friend Leslie Greenberg. "She didn't take herself seriously. She laughed at life, even though she faced dangers. She was a person without an ego. Everybody loved her. She was a bright, loyal friend. She expressed her emotions. You could call her at midnight. She would sign her notes, 'I love you always.'"

Says her first cousin, Heidi Lemish, "Ina was unique. She was the most happy person, joking, making funny noises. She was always smiling and she never complained. You never heard boo. She was happy-go-lucky. She was the brightest of the whole family. She was good at everything."

Sarah became familiar with the Children's Hospital of Eastern Ontario, especially the emergency room. Doctors and nurses recognized her. She was a regular at the gift shop, where she bought something for Ina every day that Ina was hospitalized. Usually Ina would receive a stuffed animal; teddy bears were her favorite. This was a rough life for a girl who just wanted to be normal.

It was tough on Sarah too.

Sarah would say, Ina, maybe you shouldn't eat that.

Don't tell me what to eat, Ina would reply. You seem tired, Sarah would say, why don't you lie down? Ina would respond: I know when I need to lie down.

Ina's doctor at the Children's Hospital suggested Ina needed help. He felt she wasn't facing up to the reality of her disease and booked her with a psychologist. Her parents begged her to go. They said they weren't getting any younger. They told Ina she needed to look after herself better. Reluctantly, Ina agreed to go to one appointment. Sarah vividly recalls her daughter exiting that appointment like a madwoman.

"She said, 'If you think I'm going back…I'm as completely normal as anybody and I definitely do not need help and I am not going back ever.'"

Sarah and Arnie did what they could. They drove to Ogdensburg, New York to buy sugar-free pop and sugar-free bubblegum, before such items were available in Canada. As well, Dr. Bratten, an endocrinologist at the Ottawa Civic Hospital, was trying out a new insulin pump on an experimental basis, and the Swedlers were interested in one for Ina. With the pump, which is now common, insulin is constantly infused into the abdominal area, giving a more constant flow and hopefully better control. "Oh no," Sarah says. "Ina wasn't going on the pump. She didn't want the pump." Ina didn't want to wear something bulky that had to be taken off for swimming; she thought needles were easier. When Ina was 14 years old, Sarah bought her one of the first models of glucometers, an instrument that measures the sugar in a drop of blood retrieved from a finger pinprick.

Before glucometers, diabetics tested their urine for sugar, which isn't as accurate. They had to go to a clinic to get their blood tested. Sarah paid over six hundred dollars for the foot-long machine. These days, glucometers can fit in the palm of a hand. Everyone with diabetes uses one. Did Ina use her glucometer? Now and then, says Sarah, rolling her eyes.

Sarah turned to Dr. Bratten for advice on coping with Ina's difficult attitude.

He said, "Go to Parliament and throw yourself off the top of the Peace Tower and it will make no difference. There has to be a reason for her to want to do it herself."

And there was a reason, much later on. When she was pregnant, Ina tested her blood sugar four times a day, gave herself insulin injections four times a day, and ate exactly what she should have been eating. She had perfect diabetic control, and Josh was born healthy.

When Ina was diagnosed, meticulous sugar control wasn't seen to be as important as it is today. The philosophy then was to keep out of trouble, try to avoid the hospital, don't let the blood sugar get too high or too low. Surprisingly, it took until the early 1980s (with the release of the results of the Diabetes Control and Complications Trial) to prove that tight sugar control would prevent complications like kidney disease down the road. When Ina was an adult, she confessed to a friend that if she had known this before, she would have been more careful.

Careful or not, the truth was that Ina was a brittle diabetic. Unfortunately, she had a bad case of diabetes.

Some teens who were even less careful than Ina wouldn't end up in hospital as many times as she did. Ina had bad luck her entire life. She came down with measles even though she had been immunized against the disease, and had to be hospitalized for this on her twelfth birthday. One summer, Harley, who was a counselor at camp, phoned home in a panic with alarming news. Ina had been found almost comatose lying on a bathroom floor. Sarah was in Montreal visiting her father, who was ill, so Arnie took the call from Harley and sped up to camp. Ina was lying in the camp infirmary on an intravenous drip containing sugar. It turns out the camp doctor thought Ina had low blood sugar when in fact her blood sugar was too high, and giving her more sugar was the last thing she needed. Arnie and Harley rushed Ina to the hospital, where she stayed for a week. She didn't open her eyes for the first two days. Harley visited her in hospital a few times with some buddies. (A nurse gave surgeons' uniforms to the boys, as they were planning to put on the play *One Flew Over the Cuckoo's Nest* at camp.) After the crisis had passed, Ina wrote Harley a letter of thanks. I guess you thought I was dying, she wrote.

In the meantime, Sarah became more and more involved in the diabetes cause. She and a friend, Laura Greenberg, kick-started the Canadian Diabetes Association. Before, the association was so low-key it was awful, says Sarah. It provided brochures and that was about it. The women got a phone number listed and rented an office that also acted as a drop-in centre, where people could buy needles and insulin. Gradually, more and more volunteers joined. Sarah was the fundraiser. She raised $6,000 merely by sending letters to people in the Jewish community. She organized huge fundraising dinners at the Château Laurier, featuring local and international diabetes experts. She brought in a speaker from the Joslin Clinic in Boston, a place where Ina would later spend a week. Sarah helped plan a fundraising picnic for diabetes at Vincent Massey Park. Sarah, Arnie and Ina attended this picnic, and as Arnie was lifting a crate of oranges and a crate of apples out of his car trunk, Ina insisted on leaving. The picnic had barely begun. Ina was so insistent about leaving that Arnie simply delivered the donated food and drove off with his wife and daughter.

"I was very, very involved and she couldn't care less," Sarah says. "Ina never wanted to be a part of it, never, never, never. She didn't care what I did, how I ran, how many times I went; she would have no part of it. I always thought she was in denial."

Throughout her life, Ina never complained about her diabetes, and that was also her way. Friend after friend and cousin after cousin say the same thing. Ina never complained. She didn't complain about the ugly abscesses on her head, and she never complained when she vomited day after day, and she didn't complain when she pierced her toughened skin with needles. Some people make their illness the focus of their lives. Ina didn't. The sick role didn't appeal to her. She fooled many people, complaining so little that acquaintances didn't even know she had diabetes. In fact, many of her closest friends weren't aware she was so ill. Her friend Leslie Greenberg recalls asking Ina how her trip to Florida was. Ina had gone there with her family for winter vacation. Not bad, Ina said. Later, Leslie found out that Ina had actually spent a good part of that holiday inside a hospital. Ina didn't like to burden anyone. In a way, diabetes is not the story of Ina. One friend says it's not that Ina ignored her diabetes; it's that she simply faced diabetes in her own way. Says Sarah: "She never once said 'why me?'"

Only Sarah saw her daughter's diabetes in the magnitude it ultimately was.

At age 16, Ina graduated from the the Children's Hospital. Like all teens of that age, she was forced to transfer to an adult hospital. The transition wasn't good for her. The Children's Hospital of Eastern Ontario was a new hospital where doctors wore colorful stethoscopes, where clusters of clowns could be found surrounding a child's bed. The Ottawa Civic Hospital was a rickety old place. At the Civic's diabetes clinic, Ina sat in a waiting room beside old people missing a leg or two. Patients shuffled in with white canes. Would this be *her* one day? Sometimes Ina made it to her appointments there. Sometimes she didn't.

Life moved along. Ina continued gymnastics, becoming one of the best young gymnasts in Ontario. Her coach Agnes Laing remembers she was steady on the beam, determined and focused. The bars were difficult, but the floor was where she shone, because her bubbly personality would come through. If it took Ina twenty-five tries to learn a move that should have taken only five, Ina wouldn't get frustrated. She would say, just give me a year and I'll get it. If she felt tired or wobbly, she never blamed diabetes. She'd say, excuse me, I have to sit now, I just need a couple of minutes. And when she was through with competing, she became a coach at Corona, teaching Agnes' daughter, Lianne.

Ina and her friends Lori and Donna went to a Hall & Oates concert one night when Ina was suffering from the flu. She was slick with sweat, but she didn't care. She didn't want to leave. That was her way. Even when she was on dialysis and her belly was bloated with fluid, she would hold a dinner party, or she would change into her swimming suit and drive Josh to the local pool at night. She would go cross-country skiing in forty-below weather, or she'd help organize a lunch for Hadassah, a Jewish women's fundraising group.

"Full blast ahead. One hundred per cent and you embrace. You don't hold back. You just go," says Rabbi Reuven Bulka, speaking about his congregant Ina. "You take the apples of the tree and you share them and you eat them. You just go. That was her. You don't lament the things that you don't have. You celebrate the things that you do have. She could have gotten dragged down with oy, look at me, I don't have the capacity to do everything. Instead, she said, you know what, I'll just enjoy the things that I can do and I'll do them to the full. And Ina's way was also in a large sense to do that, not in the context of a narcissistic, 'I'm going to do my own thing,' but 'I'm going to make sure I help every-body else do their thing.' Because for her the greatest pleasures in life were to have a happy environment around her, of people who were themselves happy because they were doing good things. So she was really a catalytic converter in a sense. (He shakes his head.) A rare kid."

Rabbi Bulka, of the Machzikei Hadas synagogue, is well-respected in Ottawa as a moral leader. Knowing Ina, he says, has been one of the most rare and precious blessings of his life as a rabbi. Both he and Ina worked for the same radio station in Ottawa, CFRA, having their own radio spots. Ina gave the daily business news, and Rabbi Bulka hosts his own religious phone-in show on Sunday nights. Rabbi Bulka once described Sarah's relationship with her daughter like this: "It is safe to say that Ina was actually baked into Sarah's bones."

"She was," Sarah says. "She literally was. I felt every pain she did. I felt every happiness she did. Basically for both my children but obviously because of Ina's ill-ness…she was part of me. That's why I can't get her out."

Ina's Way

Mrs. Swedler,

Ina always spoke of you as her best friend. In fact, on one of the few times that I ever saw Ina unhappy it was after a small argument that the two of you had. The difference of opinion blew over after about a day, but it was an indication to me of the extent of your closeness, that such a minor issue between you upset her so much. Ina took great joy from talking about how much you worried about her. There was no doubt in her mind about where your heart lay.

From a letter to the Swedlers by Ina's friend Steve Kahansky, written on October 5, 1996.

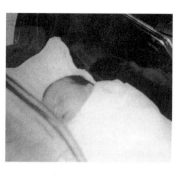

11622 SWEDLER SARAH
GIRL

FORM 164

Ottawa Civic Hospital

BABY'S NAME SWEDLER

MOTHER'S NAME SARAH- WD 4042²

SEX Girl WT. 5 lbs 4 ozs

DATE OF BIRTH Feb 23 66 TIME 12:43 AM.

RELIGION HEB BAPTISED

DOCTOR SOLOWAY

PAEDIATRICIAN GLASS

Ina with big brother Harley

1968
School Photo

At Nevele Golf & Country
Club in the Catskill Mountains.

The Swedler family taken on the occasion
of Sarah being honoured as "Outstanding
Pioneer Woman." by the Group of Pioneer
Women. Ten-year-old Ina gave a glowing
tribute to her mom at the event.

Corona Gym Club
winners. Ina, 10 years
old, is pictured at left.

Ina, right at age 14, coaching at Corona Gym Club.

Best friends at Camp B'nai B'rith, from left, Donna, Lori and Ina.

Graduation from Hillcrest High School.

Ina with her dog Hershey, taken before her high school prom.

CHAPTER 3

The Swedler Inn

Sarah grew up on Park Avenue in Montreal, on the third storey of a brick rowhouse above a lamp store. Across the street was the park Mont Royal, where she skated and tobogganed and skied with her sisters Anne and Nettie and her brother Sam. She played in Fletcher's Field and attended the Baron Byng High School. This was Mordecai Richler territory.

Her parents had immigrated from Russia during the first decade of the century. In Montreal, her father was a bag dealer, selling potato sacks. Sarah's grandmother—her mother's mother—walked to synagogue twice a day. Sarah dropped in at the synagogue at times to stand beside her grandmother and sing prayers with the pretty, slightly stooped woman.

As a teenager in the 1950s, Sarah and her girlfriends founded a group called the Deccas, named after their favorite record label. The Deccas wore flourescent red jackets (they actually glowed in the dark) and organized socials with the boys. They ate at Dunn's Deli. Sarah was known as the Karnatzel Kid, because she frequently ordered karnatzels, a kind of pepperoni stick.

Every winter, when the Santa Claus parade swept by Park Avenue, dozens of people would gather at Sarah's home, hanging over the balcony and crowding the windows and piling on the curved metal outdoor stairs to catch a glimpse of Santa and the floats. There were always people in their home, as cousins lived nearby, and they had many friends. The door was never locked. Sarah's father told his children: "Enjoy these years. It's not always going to be like this. These are truly the best years. When things get better financially, the family won't be so close."

But as an adult, Sarah was determined to maintain that close atmosphere of her childhood. She made her own home in Ottawa a gathering place, a hearth where everyone was welcome. The two busiest rooms were the kitchen and the basement. One wall in the basement was completely mirrored, so Ina and her friends could practice jazz dancing as if they were in a real studio. There was also a bar there, as big as one found in a restaurant. Ina and her friend Arlie worked on projects and studied together in the basement. The two usually received the highest marks in the class. In grade four, they wrote the *Puppy Press*, a newspaper solely about dogs. The Swedlers owned an apricot-colored poodle called Appy. (For Ina, the *Puppy Press* would be her first journalistic experience.) In the basement, Ina and her close friend Melissa Greenberg would sing together. Over and over, they rehearsed the song "The Rose," holding fake flowers and laughing their heads off because neither of them could carry a tune. Ina's friends remember with fondness the L-shaped brown velour couch. On that couch, Ina would gossip, watch TV—*Dallas* and *The Guiding Light* and *Knot's Landing* especially—and have her father tickle her feet.

"She liked to have her feet tickled all the time," says Arnie, a big teddy bear of a man. "Wherever I'd be, she'd come into the room and if I was watching TV or something she'd sit down and take her shoes off and say, 'tickle my feet.' And I always said to anybody who ever saw us doing this, that if someone was doing that to me, I'd probably be jumping out of my skin. But she didn't have any ticklish portions of her feet. From the time she was small right up to, even in the hospital. Even in the hospital when she was there in Toronto, I went to the room and I tickled her feet. She thoroughly enjoyed it."

Sarah met Arnie on a visit to Florida, when they were both almost 20 years old. Sarah had flown down for a vacation in the area now known as South Beach. Arnie was living in Florida, and had just finished a stint with the Marines. They met through mutual friends. Arnie was quiet, unlike the other American boys Sarah had met, and she liked him for that. Later, Arnie came up to Montreal to visit Sarah, and he never left, so in love was he. Interestingly, an astrologer on Jean Talon Street had predicted (before Sarah met Arnie) that Sarah would end up marrying an American. Just before the couple married, Arnie's mother phoned Sarah, and Sarah dreaded the lecture she thought she was going to get—that they were too young to marry. But her future mother-in-law simply asked Sarah this: Never ask Arnie to give up his American passport. He came from a patriotic family, and he never did relinquish his American citizenship.

Sarah and Arnie made a home together in Ottawa. They had Harley, and four years later Ina came along. (Sarah always liked the name Ina; she knew a girl in high school named Ina. Ina's middle name is Sue, after one of Sarah's grandmothers. Ina's Hebrew name is Chayah, after Arnie's grandmother. Chayah is a name that fit Ina perfectly, for it means life.)

The Swedler home was a busy home, a loud one. It wasn't unusual to have five, six, even ten additional people around the supper table. Camp days-off were the most crowded. At B'nai B'rith, counselors got one night a week off, when they were allowed to venture into the city. Ina and her friends would book off on the same night, then they'd drive back to the city along the Ottawa River and head for the three-bedroom bungalow on Linton Road. If Harley and his buddies also booked off on the same day, there could be 15 kids spending the night at the Swedlers. Sarah often made her famous refrigerator cookies, chocolate wafers layered with whipped cream. She set out bowls of Cheesies and other munchies. She fed all the friends and sat with them, joining in the gossip, taking an interest in each of them, discussing with them their boy and girl problems. That's the way it was always, a slew of kids swarming the house. Mrs. Swedler was like a second mother to some. Friends of Ina and Harley dubbed the home "The Swedler Inn." A group of kids bought Sarah a T-shirt that said "The Swedler Inn." They bought her a tulip-shaped jar printed with the words, The Swedler Inn. Sarah usually filled the jar with Hershey's Kisses.

"It was always our policy that any child who had nowhere to go would always have a place where to stay," Sarah says.

Sarah wanted her children to grow up in a home that was welcoming to others. An added bonus was that she always knew where her children were and what they were doing.

"Not that I ever worried about them. Truthfully, I worried about a lot of things, but not about the kids. I trusted them. I worried about Ina's health. I overindulged them, because they were good kids, they had good friends, they called me, they were considerate of us."

A couple of times, the socializing get out of hand. When she was in junior high, Ina invited about 15 friends over for a party. Her parents were out for the night, and knew about the party, but they didn't expect their house to be trashed. Dozens of kids heard about the party and showed up uninvited. The crashers banged on the basement walls and smashed a table. Ina couldn't believe that a bunch of rowdies had tried to destroy the house. And because Ina was crying and felt bad, Sarah felt bad for Ina.

Another incident involved a cop. Ina was interrogated by a policeman with a flashlight while she was kissing her boyfriend Mike in a parked car. Her parents weren't upset about this when they found out. Sarah found it amusing. When Arnie heard the story from a friend, he somehow concluded it was not Ina but another girl who was involved. Of course, everyone knew about the flashlight incident because Ina thought it was a good story to tell to her girlfriends the next day. Ina told stories well, adding lots of giggles. The funnier the story, the better, especially if it was a story that happened to her. And she couldn't wait to tell a story. She was like that her whole life. She needed to tell the story right after it happened, even if it meant phoning her mother at work or Harley in New York City.

Sarah has one regret about those innocent times, and it's the candy that she bought. True, she put out sugarless candy, but she also served the regular treats. She did it for Harley, mindful that he shouldn't be denied sweets because of Ina's diabetes. And Sarah figured that Ina would find candy elsewhere if she couldn't find it at home. This way, Sarah could monitor it better. Nevertheless, Sarah now asks herself if she should have done it that way. One of Ina's old friends says she feels guilty about the teenage girl pig-outs she and Ina used to have. She says she had no idea the damage it was doing.

In 1982, Ina celebrated her Sweet 16. It was a huge party. She wore a brown silky pantsuit and danced on a multi-colored disco floor. There was a Mickey Mouse cake.

Ina's friends like to tell the story of the Inuit carving. Ina was expecting a dog tag as a Sweet 16 present from Mike. All the girls wore dog tags for necklaces, engraved with their names and a little message. But Mike didn't get a dog tag for her; he bought an Inuit carving of a walrus. Harley thought it was a thoughtful, artsy gift, but Ina was miffed. She was 16 years old and she wanted a dog tag, which was considered romantic. Needless to say, the relationship didn't last. Ina did, however, become good friends again with Mike and his wife many years later. (Ina's boyfriends in her youth were either named Michael or Steven.)

Sarah has kept cards from Ina's Sweet 16. There's a oversized three-page bristol board card from Ruth Froman, complete with pictures and poems.

Ruth wrote, "I remember when we first became really close we would lie in your basement and get so depressed because we didn't have a boyfriend. We constantly wrote blackboards full of letters to G-d. I wonder why he never wrote us back. P.S. Please send us a boyfriend... Remember when we went to the NAC to see a dance performance (*Sweet Potatoe*). We laughed so hard we were crying. It's good we left in the middle because I think they would have kicked us out."

Sarah had started her own business with her friend Lillian Zunder, also a former Montrealer. They had begun as panty hose distributors, selling their product to civil servants in government offices. Later, they opened their own women's clothing store, called Her Fashions. Their store was located in a house on Bank Street, in their own neighborhood of South Ottawa. Every two weeks, Sarah and Lillian drove to Montreal to visit the clothing factories there. They picked sweaters, skirts and slacks off the racks. They had good taste, a Montreal flair, and earned loyal customers. The store was a success, although Arnie often teased Sarah by asking her how her hobby was going. Sarah would bring home thirty or forty sweaters for Ina to try on, and Ina would have her pick. Ina hated shopping at her mother's store. Ina was a Zellers' girl, as Lillian would put it, and Sarah was strictly Holt Renfrew.

Ina rarely had make-up on. She wore her hair naturally; it was shoulder-length and curly. She was down-to-earth, not fancy. Nevertheless, she had her beauty rules, rules that helped steer her girlfriends in the right direction. Rule number one, all girls need bangs. Rule number two, never, ever wear blue eyeliner, particularly if your eyes aren't blue. Melissa Greenberg just grew out her bangs last year, and she feels guilty about it because she broke Ina's number one rule.

Ina wore glasses, which suited her well. There was a time she tried to wear contacts, and her mother didn't approve. Sarah worried about infection, and she was right to worry. One time, while Ina was wearing contacts, her eyes became badly infected. Because Sarah and Arnie were out of town visiting Arnie's mother who was sick, Ina phoned Lillian.

"It was so badly infected," recalls Lillian. "It was unbelievable, really unbelievable."

Lillian could barely look at the eye. A doctor at the hospital asked for a photograph to be taken, presumably for a textbook. After that incident, Lillian could understand better how Sarah felt. She concedes that the relationship between Sarah and Ina failed in some ways because Ina couldn't cope with Sarah's worries. Then again, says Lillian, it's a mother's prerogative to worry.

As for the infected eye: "Any mother would have gone berserk, but Sarah more, because she was so devoted a mother."

Devotion isn't a strong enough word for how Sarah felt toward her children.

Lori Chazonoff, whom Ina met at B'nai B'rith, explains, "Mrs. Swedler always used to say to Ina, "You're my life," and it's so true. She was her life. They just had such a close relationship. She was her life, her little gem. I don't think Mrs. Swedler will ever be the same, ever, ever. And I would tell people, friends of mine, and they'd say, well it's like any parent, their relationship with their children, and I'd say, no, there's no comparison. You can't compare this relationship. I don't know anyone who has that type of relationship with their parents."

Sarah's relationship with Ina's son Josh is just as close. When he was two, Sarah took him to Tiny Treasures school every Friday morning. Sarah and Josh lit the candles together. They baked challah and ate it hot in the car on the way home. They sang their favorite song, "Little Torah."

Little Torah, little Torah
Let me hold you tight
Teach me, teach me
All the mitzvahs
So we'll do what's right
Torah, Torah, teaches every Jew
Torah, Torah
I love you

The High Holidays are here again and Sarah doesn't know if she has the courage to bake a honeycake. Sarah arranges the ingredients on the counter. She couldn't do it last year, or the year before. She remembers the time her honeycake flopped four times in a row on the same day. Ina watched the repeated flops, and fell to the floor laughing, not believing her mother would keep trying and trying. It's a family trait, this perseverance.

Sarah had been trying out a new recipe the year that Ina had laughed so much. It was the kind of cake that you bake for awhile, remove it from the oven, invert it, and place it back in the oven. But each time Sarah tried to invert it, the cake was pure liquid and ran all over the counter. Sarah repeated the recipe, but this time she left it in the oven for longer before inverting it, and still it ran, as if it had never felt heat. The third time she left it in the oven even longer, and it ran again. Same with the fourth time. But by the fifth time, she left it in double the amount of time called for, and it worked. There must have been something wrong with the recipe.

Sarah removes a couple of bowls from her cupboard. She stares at the flour and honey and sugar and eggs. Her son and his family are due from New York tonight. They would want honeycake for dessert. It's a tradition, representing the sweetness of the Jewish New Year. Remembering Ina's laughter over the honeycake, she fears that if she starts to make it she'll begin to cry and never stop.

There's a saying that Sarah once read a magazine, and she is reminded of it sometimes when she feels bewildered. "There is a word for a child who has lost his parents. That's an orphan. There's a word for a person who loses his spouse. That's a widow or widower. But there is no word for a parent who loses a child."

Ina's Way

How can I describe Ina and what she meant to me in words? Ina was and will always remain my best friend. She was always there to support me and give me guidance. I hope Ina knew that I was always there for her and would have done anything for her. I usually do not express my feelings in words, however, a few months ago I wrote a letter to Ina. I tried to describe exactly how I felt towards her and what she meant to me. I am so glad that I got the opportunity to do that.

Ina knew me better than even I knew myself. She was always protecting me and tried not to upset me by occasionally withholding information. She was always so concerned about how I was doing. I used to feel guilty expressing my sadness to her. It seemed that what I was going through was nothing close to what she was experiencing. I only wish that I had not burdened her with my problems over the past few months, however I know that I would never have been able to get through some of those rough times without her. She would listen and offer me not an opinion but rather help me deal with the situations and look at the positive side of things.

Lori Chazonoff, a friend.
1996

CHAPTER 4

Freedom

Ina stood in her new room in McConnell Hall at McGill University. "Isn't it gorgeous?" she sighed. "It's nicer than my room at home."

Sarah and Arnie couldn't believe what they were hearing. The room was small. It contained a bed, a desk, a cupboard and hardly any room for anything else. Harley, Ina's cousin Jeff and Ina's current boyfriend were all standing in the hall because they couldn't fit inside. But the size of the room didn't matter to Ina. She was 18 years old, and to her, Room 423 at McConnell Hall meant freedom.

"I was told this was the 'cool' residence to live in, and as I got out of the car I wondered why," wrote Ina in her story "The Undergraduates," which she composed after her first year at McGill. "I clearly remember the first thing I, as well as my horrified parents, saw as we began unloading the car. A huge, 18-wheeler truck pulled up to McConnell, and starting unloading a full load of cases of beer, directly into the main floor of my residence. They used a conveyer belt, much like the ones you see at the grocery store when you get a take-out order."

Ina had earned a $100 scholarship from Ottawa's Carleton University to study journalism, but she preferred to journey a little further from home. Most of her friends decided on the University of Toronto. Sarah thought it was too far. Ina didn't have family in Toronto then, whereas in Montreal, she had a load of aunts and uncles and cousins, including her first cousin Jeffrey Zaltzman, who also had diabetes and later became a kidney specialist in Toronto. As well, Sarah traveled to Montreal often; she and Lillian drove to Montreal once every two weeks on buying trips.

McConnell Hall was an ugly, modern building on top of a hill, backing onto Mont Royal. The cafeteria, a round building with huge windows all around, lay in the centre of all the residences. Ina didn't enjoy the food and avoided eating there. Her parents bought her a little fridge in which to keep her insulin and milk and other munchies. The residence was a short walk from where Sarah grew up, and Sarah never tired of telling Ina stories of her childhood—anecdotes about her childhood, like how she ate at Dunn's Deli and downhill-skied on Mont Royal.

Ina majored in political science at McGill. Her marks were disappointing to her. She told her mother she must have left her brain in Ottawa. She had earned an Ontario Scholarship in high school, but life at McGill was so exciting her work suffered. In Ina's words, she had a choice between her career and her social life, and she chose the latter. Ina never missed the humor in anything she did. This was her honest, biting take on academics at McGill, as told in "The Undergraduates":

In my infinite wisdom, I decided to take a basic political science course called Political Theory. It sounded interesting, all about Karl Marx, John Stuart Mill, Rousseau and the like. The four professors who intermittently taught the course, were all highly respected. The problem was, I did not understand one thing that went on in that course, and believe me, I was not alone. I distinctly remember one professor, Charles Taylor. This man is a genius, and I don't think anyone except a genius could relate to him. Everything seemed so easy for him, he probably thought we were a bunch of morons not to be able to understand him. I took two other political science courses, one which started out as a bet because my boyfriend, who was now my ex-boyfriend, said I would not be able to sit through his boring class three times a week, and if I did, he would take me out to a really expensive restaurant at the end of the year. Never one to back down from a challenge, I decided to take the course....As well as taking political science courses, I was allowed to take two other courses of my choice. I was still struggling to find a fifth, when I heard about the 'joke course' of the year. This course was offered every Monday evening, from 5:30 to 8:30. Attendance was not required, and the only thing you had to do for the course was write a five-page paper. This sounded too good to be true, so I decided to go the first lecture, on

Greek mythology. As I entered the class, I realized that I was only one of many people who had heard about the course. The room was filled with people I knew, mostly Jewish kids from summer camp. I was sitting beside an old friend of mine, when in walked the professor. Old is too mild a work to describe this teacher. The man had white hair, a cane, and looked like he was about to topple over at any given moment. But wait, he hadn't spoken yet. He slowly opened his tired mouth, and H-E-L-L-O croaked out. I was in hysterics, along with the rest of the 200 people in the room, and just hoped and prayed this man would not drop dead before the end of the term. Supposedly this man was still teaching because of a political technicality, and everyone wanted to take his course, so nobody asked any questions. Towards the end of the semester I felt guilty that I had only gone to two of his lectures, so I went to a class. There were only four other people there.

And this was her take on Welcome Week and residence life:

I had been drunk once before in my life, and it only took two 'zombies' to get me that way. This time I had about seven drinks, I don't even remember what they were, and I was flying pretty high. We went to a bar downtown, called Christopher's, and told the bartender it was our birthdays. He seemed to believe us, and decided we deserved free drinks. After getting pretty silly, we decided we needed food badly, so we ventured over to Burger King at 4 a.m. By the time we left BK, the entire restaurant, which was filled with Shriners, was chanting my name, which I told them was Sue (my middle name) as we left. I think we were all proposed marriage to on that night. Before I lose myself in all the funny stories that went on during those years, let me tell you about myself at that time. I was 18, and a pretty likeable person. I am a diabetic, and was very prone to infections, especially since I got diabetes at the age of ten. Being in the university atmosphere, which included drinking and numerous pig-outs, I was not in the best control as far as my health was concerned. I mean, let's face it, I didn't want to miss out on anything at that point in my life....Anyhow, one weekend, Jen's boyfriend of over a year, Jon, was coming up to visit her from Boston. [Jen was a friend who lived on Ina's floor at McConnell.] She had told him all about me, and vice versa, and we were all looking forward to having a good weekend. The first of one of my many strange illnesses happened. I had been having pains in my neck all week long and I felt a small bump on my head. I had been blow drying my hair one day, and had accidentally hit my head with the blow dryer, so I figured that was the resulting bump....Finally, the day Jon came to Montreal I couldn't take the pain anymore, so I went to the emergency room at the Royal Victoria Hospital. I'm a very private person, and I don't like to complain, so I went alone, without telling any of my friends, my two cousins who were doctors, or my parents, since I didn't want to worry anyone. When I returned to residence about four hours later, my entire head was wrapped in gauze bandages. I won't describe to you what they did to me there, but suffice to say that I had an abscess about the size of a fist on my head, which had to be removed. I left the hospital with literally a hole in my head. When I returned to residence, not only did I look like a mummy who had just been crying and screaming for the past three hours, but everyone was looking for me to see where I was. That was when I met Jon, and hoped that he had left his glasses at home. Unfortunately for me, he didn't wear glasses. I'm not a vain person but this was ridiculous. I immediately ran into my room, grabbed a picture of myself and said, 'This is what I really look like.' From that day on, my friends in residence who had seen me that day always teased me by saying I had a big head.

Ina, Jen O'Malley and another friend named Joni rented an apartment together during their second and third years at McGill. It was located on Durocher Street, in the so-called "student ghetto." To sign the lease, they needed parental signatures, so Ina's parents came in from Ottawa. Jennifer remembers that as Sarah and Arnie ascended the stairs to check out the apartment with the landlord, they started speaking Yiddish to one another. When Ina noticed this, she worried her parents thought the place a bit of a dump, and she turned to Jen and whispered, "Now we're in trouble."

As well, the apartment was on the fourth floor, a fact that concerned Arnie. Arnie regularly brought Ina boxes of diet drinks and salamis and sugarless candy, and he didn't know how he'd be able to carry them up to the top floor.

Ina's response was, "What did you want me to do? Get an apartment with a doorman?"

Ina was so comfortable with Joni and Jennifer that she injected her insulin at the kitchen table in front of them. When injecting, diabetics need to rotate their sites to prevent tissue damage. They inject insulin into their arms, legs and abdomen, and they alternate the site each time. Needles were a fact of life for Ina, not a big deal. Looking back, Jennifer says that Ina wanted to live her life in a normal way, but also respected diabetes as a force in her life. In Ina's heart of hearts, Jennifer adds, Ina knew that Sarah's promptings regarding health were ultimately for her own good.

With both children gone, Sarah suffered from "empty mother syndrome," as only she would phrase it. Ina was in Montreal, Harley was studying architecture in Rome. After enjoying all those kids roaming through her house for years, Sarah found the adjustment difficult. Says Sarah, "Someone once said to me, 'Don't get too close to your children.' I said, 'How could you ever say that?' But maybe it's true."

Sarah phoned Ina every day at McGill, often at ten or five or three minutes to six at night. Since the cheap rates began at 6 p.m., Ina couldn't understand why Sarah didn't wait the few extra minutes.

"Mom, do you realize what time it is?" she would ask.

That was another cute one, Sarah says now. Sarah truly could not wait those few extra minutes.

Meanwhile, Sarah was growing increasingly worried about Ina's diabetes. She didn't like the way Ina was caring for herself. Ina frequently changed doctors at the Civic. This one was too old. That one was too young.

"We were going from doctor to doctor," Sarah says. "I didn't know if we were on the right path. I just didn't feel comfortable about the way we were running."

So, just after Ina's first year at McGill and before Ina's summer trip to Israel, Sarah arranged for Ina to spend a week at the Joslin Clinic in Boston, a world-renowned centre for diabetes. This news didn't go over well with Ina.

"I said, 'Ina, we're getting on a plane tomorrow, you and me and dad, and we're going to the Joslin Clinic.' Well, the ceiling went, the whole house went. She says, 'why?' She didn't speak to me. She was angry and it was just awful, she was packing to move out of the house, she was going to leave forever. I said, 'Ina, it's just a precaution, it's because you're feeling well now.' Anyhow, we got her on the plane, I don't remember how. The whole world knew what a horrible parent I was. Even my husband wasn't for it. And nobody was in the family. What am I going to gain, the medical people said. What are you looking for? Arnie said she feels good, she has no problems. But she did have problems at McGill. When she had that thing on her head, and how many other things I didn't know about. Believe me, I found out after. She didn't tell me a lot of things. If I didn't take her to the Joslin, I felt that I hadn't done everything I could possibly do in my life for her."

Ina didn't speak to her parents on the plane. From the airport in Boston, they headed to the Children's Inn, where they would all stay the first night. It was raining. At about 4 p.m., Ina said she wanted to go out for a walk. Three hours later, she hadn't returned. Arnie and Sarah went looking for her. Sarah was convinced her daughter had flagged down a taxi, escaped to the airport, and returned home. (Ina had her own credit card.) Her parents were going out of their minds. Sarah was just about to phone the police when they spotted Ina crying, her head in her hands, on the wet steps of Harvard Medical School.

"This was the first time I saw my husband put up his hand as if he was going to hit her," Sarah says. "He was so frightened."

A food wagon stood in front of the Children's Inn. Arnie bought some food there for supper, but Ina refused to eat. Sarah feared Ina would collapse.

The next day, relations between Ina and her parents did not improve. As Sarah was registering Ina at the Joslin Clinic, Ina disappeared down a tunnel that led back to the Children's Inn. Arnie followed her and sternly told her to return to the clinic.

Ina did so, then told her parents, "This is where you're taking me. This is what you're doing to me."

Sarah was beside herself. Her heart was breaking. When they had finished registering, they took a look around. There were a lot of young patients, all dressed in regular clothes. Right in front of them, a young man collapsed, presumably from a diabetic coma. Said Ina: "What a welcome. I'm going to be next." Ina's roommate at the Joslin was a girl her age, a wild kid who made no secret of the fact that she used drugs.

"Am I like that?" Ina asked her mother. "Do I have be here?"

Says Sarah now, "She couldn't get a normal roommate?"

During the week, Ina mostly lay in bed and read, attended lectures on diabetes, and underwent numerous medical tests of her eyes, her urine, her blood. Arnie wanted to take her to a baseball game at Fenway Park. She refused, so he went alone, getting lost on his way back.

The doctors at the Joslin Clinic discovered a problem with Ina's eyes, and advised her to monitor the problem after she returned home. This was the first time such an abnormality was noticed in Ina. Diabetes damages the blood vessels in the back of the eyes. New vessels pop up to take their place, but these new ones aren't strong and bleed easily. It's called diabetic retinopathy, and it causes blindness in diabetics. In fact, not long after Ina had returned from the Joslin Clinic, she had two laser eye treatments at the Ottawa Civic Hospital. The treatment killed the new blood vessels before they had a chance to bleed, and thus saved Ina's eyesight. Ina's friend Donna recalls sitting in the waiting room with Sarah during those laser treatments. Ina had asked her friend to do this, for the sole purpose of comforting her mother.

The Joslin Clinic also noticed protein in her urine, a sign of kidney disease. The significance of kidney problems was not lost on Sarah. Sarah thought about dialysis, and a feeling of dread passed through her.

Sarah's sister Annie flew in to Boston to keep Sarah company at the Joslin Clinic because Arnie had to return to his business after the first several days. Ina was in no mood to socialize. She didn't speak to Annie. She still wasn't speaking to Sarah, either. By now, Sarah was getting a little irritated at her daughter. Sarah was now convinced she had done the right thing by bringing Ina to Boston. The Joslin clinic doctors had noticed the eye damage and they had found protein in her urine. They also put Ina on twice-daily insulin injections. Previously, she had been taking insulin once a day in the morning, which was the norm then.

After a week, Ina's stay at the Joslin ended. As Ina, Sarah and Annie were waiting for a cab outside the clinic that would take them to the airport, Ina smiled at her mother and said, "You know, Mom, this wasn't such a bad place after all. I may come back in a year or two. They give you your freedom, you know. It's the best place for me."

Sarah stared at her. "I said, 'Thank you, Ina, that's very nice, after what you put me through, that's very nice.' And Ina laughed and got on the plane like nothing happened, and she started getting ready for Israel."

Incredibly, Sarah wasn't worried about Ina's trip to Israel in 1985. The first reason was that Donna was going on the trip, and Donna was very responsible. Second, the Zunders happened to be visiting Israel at the time, and Ina planned to join them for a couple of days. Ina's trip was an organized one for teens, partly spent on a kibbutz (a socialist farming community), partly spent touring the country. Harley teased his mother, saying she felt so comfortable about Ina going to Israel when they were "bombing all over the place." Sarah, however, felt as if she could "reach out and touch" her daughter while she was in Israel. Ina phoned at least once a week, sometimes three times a week, whenever she could get an operator. And the trip would be a momentous one for Ina, because she was to be bat-mitzvahed at the Western Wall.

Ina kept a diary on her trip. Her first entries read: "The date of departure finally arrived. Mom, Dad and Har drove me to Mirabel. I slept all the way. Said goodbye and cried, but I kept saying, 'I'm really happy!' Left Mirabel at about 4:00. Everyone on the trip seems really nice. We all talked on the plane, slept for about an hour. Miss mom and dad already. Flight was long, meal was bad. Landing was great. What a feeling to see Israel…Israel is beautiful. It is a cool, breezy day! Went straight to Kibbutz Gevim. It's no luxury hotel, that's for sure! Ate lunch at the dining room—yummy. I'm anticipating great weight loss on Kibbutz, whether I like it or not. Really nice pool here. We don't start working until Sunday."

Then, in a different colored pen, she writes: "Correction, Donna and I start working in the dining room tomorrow, at 7:00. Donna fell through her chair at the pool this afternoon, all the Israeli kids laughed at her, it was pretty hysterical....Things are looking better except for the living facilities, one bathroom for 12, 1 sink, no pillow or blanket. Oh well, such is life."

Ina worked a variety of jobs on the kibbutz. She mopped the floors in the dining room, peeled onions, weeded cotton fields, and threw watermelons onto trucks, mostly in the early morning before the sun became too hot. It was hard work, a world away from the relatively easy ways of home, but Ina seemed to relish it.

A sampling of Ina's kibbutz diary gives an idea of what her life was like there:

> *June 21: Hi! Woke up at 7:15 a.m., started working in the dining hall at 8:30 a.m. until 1:30 p.m. It was good—set tables for shabbat, cleaned, mopped etc. Mom would have laughed. Went to pool this aft, then walked over to a school to try to phone mom. Phone on kibbutz is broken, so was school phone. Hope mom isn't too worried. Just had a small pre-shabbat service with the group. My first shabbat in Israel, it's very exciting. Slept for 1 hour this aft. Feet sore from standing all day.*
>
> *June 24: Worked in the cotton fields. It was hot*

but not too bad. Started at 5:30, weeding. Got filthy. French fries for lunch, they were great. I'm so tired!

June 25: Woke up at 4:30 even though I had a fever and didn't have to work, felt I had to call home. Bubbie died. I felt awful. Mom sounded like she was holding up well. I miss Mom and Dad a lot! Didn't work that day. At 1:00 we went to Jerusalem for a day trip. Went to Mount of Olives, it is beautiful. Saw Hebrew U, Dome of the Rock. We walked along the wall from the Armenian quarter to the Jewish quarter. We went to the wall, I put a note in. It was really nice, not as emotional as I thought it would be, maybe because I was sick. Went downtown Ben Yehuda St. for about 2 and a half hours, it was so nice. Sat at an outdoor cafe. Walked around. It's very modern. Took pictures of Israeli soldiers. Headed back to Gevim at about 9:00. I finally felt like I was in Israel. Kibbutz life is really hard work. Only one week has gone by.

June 26: Didn't work today, had 104 fever. Slept and drank. Dr. gave me some pills. Everyone was very concerned, especially Donna. Took good care of me.

June 27: Didn't work again today, but yahoo no more fever. Felt 1000000 times better. Went to the pool all afternoon. Met Giddi, really nice guy, his hair is longer than Donna's, we measured in the pool. Saw the cutest puppy Baruch. At nite Harley called me, I was so happy. Had a bonfire sang etc and had disco in the bomb shelter!

June 28: Worked in 'the garden' with Jon. On Friday 'the garden' means acting as garbagemen. Jon and I rode on a tractor and threw garbage on top of it. I wore a tank top and Jon said he could see my white bits (he's from England!) Also said he likes how I bounce! Got cleaned up and ready for free weekend in Tel Aviv. Finally found the road and a hotel, the Florida Inn. Not luxurious, better than Kibbutz though. The beach is soooo beautiful.

After Ina had finished touring Israel with her group, she and Donna decided to fly to Greece for a week:

Aug. 7: Well I must say this has been a very peculiar day! We landed in Athens in great spirits, checked our bag for the week, changed our ticket for home and came to a beautiful hotel, the ELEC-TRA. We went out and walked around in Athens and to our dismay everyone said there is absolutely no way we will ever find a place to stay on any island because it is totally packed here. We were upset and didn't know where to go, so I phoned home to tell Sarah I arrived safely, and she told me where Ian (Zunder) was staying in Mikanos. We decided to go there and were really happy at that point. We went to the Acropolis, which was totally incredible, what a view! Came back to hotel and decided to try to call and make a reservation at the same place as Ian. It was impossible to find a room anywhere etc. DEVASTATION set in! Called back and found a room so it looks like we are going to Mikanos tomorrow, by boat. I'm happy! Yahooo!!! This day has been tres stressful, emotionally draining and we're functioning on 2 hours of sleep! I put polish on my toenails! Sexy!

During the next two summers, Ina took organized bus trips out west, first as a camper, then as a counselor. During these trips, she camped in Canada and the United States. Ina was usually very careful with her diabetes during her travels. She often stayed in isolated areas, and knew that if she ran into trouble it would be difficult to get treatment quickly. Giving herself needles and eating at the proper times wasn't easy while sleeping in a tent and being constantly on the move, but Ina managed to do it well. She stayed healthy during her Kon Tiki tour of Europe in the summer of 1988, in which she visited 18 countries by bus. One unfortunate misunderstanding occurred on this trip. Sarah remembers how Ina phoned home one day, telling her and Arnie that she was about to board a boat to a Greek island and gave the name of the island. She added that she would not be able to call for three days. The next day's news told of a terrorist attack on a boat with the same name as the island. Sarah, upset, mistakenly assumed Ina was on the boat, and was hysterical, crying, phoning the Canadian embassy, trying to gain any information she could. Her sisters drove in from Montreal to comfort her and Arnie. Meanwhile, Ina was happily lounging on a Greek island, unaware of the chaos back home. After several days, when Ina phoned home again, Sarah and Arnie demanded that she fly home right away. Ina said, "If you make me come home I'm getting a lawyer."

Ina didn't fly home, of course. She would live her life her way.

Ina's Way

Ina McCarthy joined the Young Women's Leadership Council two years ago when her son Josh was nine weeks old. Ina came into our midst, reached out and touched our hearts.

Two days before her surgery she attended a UJA canvasser training session. Two days after her surgery she asked her mom to find her book at home with her cards because she wanted to do them right away. That was Ina.

Few, if any of us knew what she had been through—and it is only now when we look back that we can appreciate her courage and the power and the joy to be found in living each moment in life to the fullest...as she did.

I went to visit Ina last Sunday. She is buried a few feet from my brother who died at the age of 27. Ina was 30 years old. She should not have died. I have learned that in life, there are no easy answers. We were fortunate to know her and our hearts go out to the entire family.

I think Ina was a woman who believed—the clouds that cover the sunshine could not banish the sun. Ina was a woman who reached a place in life that seemed impossible to go over, under or around—so she went through—and her indomitable spirit, grace and enthusiasm to live life the "Ina

Way" was a victory for her and an inspiration to us all.

We will always remember Ina with admiration, love and affection. May her memory be a blessing.

Written by Linda Nadolny-Cogan, read at a meeting of the Young Women's Leadership Council on October 10, 1996.

CHAPTER 5

Parades and Matzah Ball Soup

No matter where Sarah was, whether she was at home or in the car or at the dry cleaners or shopping for clothes, she would ensure the radio was tuned onto CFRA 580 AM at 4:35 p.m. That's when Ina's voice would cross the airwaves with her daily business report. "My daughter's on the radio in a couple of minutes," she would say. "Do you mind changing the station?" Then Sarah would listen carefully, not to the price of stocks or to the details of the latest merger, but to the tone of her daughter's voice. The voice told Sarah whether Ina was sick or well. If Sarah hadn't seen Ina in a couple of days, she would listen even more carefully. Was the voice sparkly or tired-sounding? Was Ina as funny as usual, or less so? Did she sound like she had just woken up? Was she making her report from home or from the office? When Ina realized that her mother was monitoring her well-being in this way, she tried to sound upbeat when she wasn't feeling well. Still, it was difficult to fool Sarah Swedler.

"She always knew that I knew," Sarah says.

Ina became a successful journalist by working hard and paying her dues.

It was after her graduation from McGill University that she decided to be a reporter. She had applied to Carleton University's journalism school after high school, but turned down her acceptance because she wanted to leave Ottawa. After McGill, she mailed an application to the journalism program at Ryerson University in Toronto, and wasn't accepted. She ended up spending a year in the journalism program at Algonquin College, yet even with a diploma, it was tough to find a job at a newspaper. She sent her resume across the country, but had no luck. Some of her friends were waitressing at the Southside Diner, across from the Blue Heron Mall and owned by a friend of Ina's named Steven. Her friends were making good money there. Ina thought about waitressing herself. Her mother was not enthused.

"Well," Sarah said, "a waitress?"

"Why, are you too snobby?" Ina asked.

Sarah remembers the arguments over this. "She kept talking about it, and she knew that the more she talked about it, the more it aggravated me. It was hard work, waitressing, I'm thinking, how is she going to get through this? At least a month she wasn't working. It looks like so much fun, she says. I say, you graduated from McGill, you were a top student, you're going to be a waitress. Go work for dad. Oh, no, that was even worse. Thank goodness she got a call from the Carleton Place newspaper. And that was another worry for me, her driving back and forth in the winter."

Ina finally landed a job at a small-town newspaper

called the *Carleton Place Canadian* in 1988. Carleton Place is located about a half-hour west of Ottawa. Ina rented a basement apartment in the town. Sarah visited the place and shuddered when she saw it. She thought Ina's apartment on Durocher Street in Montreal was bad, but at least it was near the place of her own childhood.

Ina was so adaptable, Sarah says. She accepted living in a pretty crummy place. Furnishings were sparse—there was no headboard on her bed, for instance. Ina didn't mind. As it turns out, Ina spent more time sleeping at her old home on Linton than in Carleton Place anyway. It wasn't so far away after all, Sarah admits now. Several times, when Sarah was expecting a visit from her daughter, she would get into her car and drive the route that Ina would take, but in the opposite direction, hoping she would pass Ina on the road and know that Ina had made it into the city safely before she actually arrived.

One night, Sarah drove to Carleton Place carrying a full dinner for two. Ina was on duty at the paper that night, busy listening to the police scanner. If she heard anything newsworthy, such as a fire or robbery, she had to rush out to cover it. That one night, her mother entered the newsroom loaded down with dishes of chicken and potatoes, diet drinks, and Ina's favorite food at the time—salad. The meal filled the newsroom with the aroma of homestyle cooking. Ina wasn't expecting her mother and told her she didn't have to do this for her. "I have nothing to do, Ina," Sarah told her. "What do I have to do?" The two dined together with the static of the scanner as their background music.

As a news assignment at the *Carleton Place Canadian*, Ina covered the Santa Claus parade in a rural town called Almonte. When Sarah heard about this assignment, she remembered the Santa Claus parades on Park Avenue that she had watched from her home as a child, and she asked Ina if she could accompany her. You don't mind, Ina asked. Of course not, Sarah answered. Sarah felt an attachment to Almonte. Sarah's parents had lived in Almonte for a year when they were newlyweds managing a small dry goods store before they settled in Montreal.

The day of the parade was bright and cold. Mother and daughter teamed up to cover the story. Ina scratched out notes on a small pad, while Sarah barked her observations. The parade's coming! Two RCMP policemen are leading it! A decorated milk truck! Horses are coming! Santa and his sled! Ina madly wrote down the details. The whole thing lasted about five minutes. When it was over, the crowd remained, for reasons unknown to Sarah and Ina. Everyone waited a bit, standing around. Then the two RCMP officers appeared again around the corner.

"Mom!" Ina shouted. "It's coming around twice!"

Sure enough, the parade passed by twice. Sarah and Ina burst out laughing. They then ran to a restaurant to get warm and finish making the notes together.

"We had so many laughing times," Sarah says now sadly.

Ina gradually got better and better reporting jobs. After about a year in Carleton Place, Ina was hired for a part-time job at the *Ottawa Citizen* newspaper, a major daily. Then, after she married Stuart, she was hired on full-time at the *Ottawa Sun*, where he worked. At the *Sun*, Ina excelled, winning the prestigious Edward Dunlop Award of Excellence for stories on welfare fraud. Her business reporting experience allowed her to get a job as a reporter at the *Ottawa Business Journal*, a weekly newspaper. She worked there after she gave birth to Josh, and was able to continue working from home for the *Journal* while she waited to be beeped for her kidney-pancreas transplant.

Ina's boss at the *Ottawa Business Journal* was Mark Sutcliffe, who also hosted the afternoon radio show on CFRA every day. The short business report on his show, care of the *Ottawa Business Journal*, was done by Ina. Once, during Mark and Ina's banter, which usually preceded the actual business update, Mark mentioned to Ina that he was sick with a cold. Ina suggested he try her mother's matzah ball soup. What's matzah ball soup, he asked, and Ina, giggling, explained. How do I make matzah ball soup, he asked, but Ina didn't know exactly. Then a friend of Ina's called the show from his cell phone, with advice for Mark on how to make matzah balls. Sarah was sitting at home listening to all of this, laughing out loud. Later she asked Ina, "How could you not know how to make matzah ball soup?"

Sarah will admit now that when Ina first started on the radio, she phoned up a manager at the station, saying how much she liked Ina's business report. She encouraged her friends to do the same. Of course, the station never knew that some of the praise for Ina came from Ina's mother and her mother's friends.

As a reporter, Ina loved people stories. She enjoyed the human drama of someone starting a business and making it fly. When the journal changed its format, Ina scooped the competition in its first new issue with the story that Beaver Tails was planning to set up a stand at Disney World. (Beaver Tails, originating in Ottawa, makes the popular deep-fried pastries in the shape of a beaver's tail.) According to Mark Sutcliffe, Ina was also one of the first journalists to write an article about the cookbook *LooneySpoons*. Sarah often offered Ina story ideas, which Ina didn't always use. For example, Sarah gave some furniture and clothes to the Canadian Diabetes Association because the group was joining other charities in a sale to raise money. A few days later, Sarah's hairdresser shopped at the sale and noticed a lawn chair with the name Swedler written on the back of it. Sarah heard about this while getting her hair tinted. Her hairdresser added that the store was also selling used underwear. Sarah phoned Ina immediately, suggesting her daughter do a story on the sale. ("I was her best resource," Sarah says.) With Sarah still on the phone, Ina called out to her colleagues, filling them in on the story her mother wanted her to write.

"Everybody here is in hysterics," Ina told her mother. "I can't believe they sell used underwear." Ina didn't do the story.

"Ina was the life of our office," wrote Mark in 1996 in an article about Ina. "She was the first to suggest a staff lunch to honor a birthday or anniversary. She was the first to bring a group together so she could tell a story, even if the humor was at her own expense. Her 30th birthday, a day many would play down or hide, was heavily promoted in advance by Ina as an event for all of us to celebrate. Ina wasn't in the office every day—she was a part-time employee who sometimes worked from home—but if you hadn't seen her for a few days, it wasn't unusual for her to greet you as if it had been months. 'Any gossip today?' she would ask slyly and in mocked hushed tones. If you said no, she would respond, with her voice rising, 'Make something up!' She was an award-winning business journalist, but what was unique about Ina's writing was how much it reflected her good nature and optimism. She was capable of getting the information she needed for a news story and was not afraid of asking questions. But she was not the stereotypical tough, aggressive, confrontational journalist. She wrote dozens of profiles of local business executives which focused on the happiness in their personal lives, and their relationships with their families. As her editor, I often asked her to include more about business in her profiles. Thinking back now, I realize how much her stories reflected her genuine interest in other people's happiness. Though our mandate might have been to cover business, Ina was in journalism to meet, talk to, learn about, and write about people."

Mark remembers how one day, Ina parked her car in the lot beside the office of the *Journal*. A man approached her and asked for five dollars. She gave the man a $20 bill and waited for her change. Next thing she knew, the man was gone. Ina thought it was hilarious that she had just been ripped off, never mind that she had lost twenty dollars. As usual, Ina saw the humor in the situation, instead of feeling sorry for herself.

What is the legacy of Ina? She was a regular person, a humorous person, a kind person, a talented journalist, a loyal daughter, a good friend, a wonderful wife, a dedicated mother, and least of all, a diabetic. Those who knew her found her to be an inspiration.

"Ina's life shows you that no grand schemes are necessary to make a difference in the world," Mark says. "You don't need to be the leader of a political party. You don't need to lead some human rights movement. You don't need to discover a cure for something. Not that all those things aren't of benefit, but there's an opportunity for every person, in a series of small ways, to make a difference in other people's lives, without some grandiose scheme, and that was one of the most powerful lessons of Ina's life. It was just a matter of caring for other people and talking to them and listening to them, and it sounds so simple, but there are so many people, particularly in our complicated modern world, who are striving for some big goal that will be their legacy. The legacy that Ina built that is lasting in so many people is, a little bit every day, building quality relationships with other human beings and caring about them."

Ina's Way

We bellied up to the bar and ordered up a big platter of fattening bar food and a couple of Diet Cokes, settling in to catch up on each other's lives. We chatted, the way women do, about our hectic schedules, bouncing between work and home. Our husbands (we both married journalists), our jobs, her toddler's toilet-training exploits, the newspaper business. She mentioned she'd gone to lunch that week with a young woman I knew who was just starting out as a reporter at a small paper and was having trouble making ends meet. "I felt so bad," she said. "She couldn't afford lunch, so she just ordered coffee. We went to this place downtown that has these great big sandwiches. I couldn't possibly eat the whole thing, so I gave her half my sandwich. I could tell she was just starving! She was so grateful—it was the least I could do." It was a sweet, simple story, one of the dozens of anecdotes told that evening amid all the laughing and drinking.

From "The Ina Way," a column written by Linda Williamson of the *Ottawa Sun* in the fall of 1996.

CHAPTER 6

The Miracle of Josh

Stuart McCarthy picked up the *Ottawa Citizen* one morning and saw a picture of his future bride.

Ina had written an article about Rosh Hashanah for the paper. In the photograph, she was preparing dough for knishes with her mother.

"I can always smell the Jewish New Year coming," the article began, "All through the house there's the smell of fresh bread, and the honey that is symbolic of a sweet year to come….While the holiday stressed repentance, I never remember it being a sad time, but one filled with love. And it is a time for sharing."

This was a newspaper article that changed Ina's life.

Stuart wanted to meet the woman who wrote so beautifully about a tradition she cherished. He phoned Maria Bohuslawksy, a former colleague who worked as a reporter at the *Citizen*, where Ina worked. Stuart and Maria knew each other because both had been reporters at the *Toronto Sun* and the *Winnipeg Free Press*. Now, Stuart was a senior reporter at the *Ottawa Sun*, recently moved from Winnipeg, and single. He asked Maria about Ina, whether she was also single, whether Maria could arrange for him to meet her. Maria said she would speak to Ina.

Ina was already seeing someone, and it was left at that. Then, a few weeks later, Ina sheepishly approached Maria, explaining she was now available. Maria organized an evening at the Ritz restaurant with a group of friends. Among those invited were Ina and Stuart. After supper, the group danced at Chez Henri. Ina and Stuart danced together, and that was the beginning of their romance. "You could just see there was an immediate click," Maria says.

The couple went out constantly. They were quick-witted with each other, ribbing each other, laughing a lot. Ina made fun of her own hair, her weight, her thighs, and Stuart just looked at her and cracked up. Ina asked her friends, doesn't he look like Tom Selleck? In fact, Stuart was older than Ina by seven years. He wore a moustache. He was also reserved, and Sarah wasn't used to that.

"She liked that he was different," says Sarah. "He had control. She liked to be taken care of."

When Sarah heard the name Stuart McCarthy, she was a little shocked. McCarthy wasn't a Jewish name, and Sarah didn't believe that Stuart was Jewish, even though Ina assured her that he was. Sarah, like many Jewish mothers, felt it important that their children marry within the faith. Even when Stuart showed up at the Swedlers for his first Friday night dinner, wearing a kipa and reciting a Hebrew prayer, Sarah refused to believe that he was Jewish. She thought they were fooling her. Stuart had lived on a kibbutz for a year, but many people who aren't Jewish live on kibbutzim. Finally Harley told his mother: "Why would anyone want to say he's a Jew when it's so hard to be a Jew?"

Only then was Sarah convinced.

Stuart learned all he could about diabetes. In fact, while they were courting, Stuart wrote a page-long article for the *Ottawa Sun* about diabetes, with the headline, "Walking a Life Line."

The article began, "For Juliette Chatterjee, diabetes is a life or death balancing act. New advances in diabetes research may one day allow Chatterjee to throw away her lifeline—a tiny insulin pump hooked into her abdomen. But for now, she and many of the other 30,000 diabetics in the Ottawa area must continually walk a fine line controlling blood sugar levels."

The story went on to explain islet cell transplants, still an experimental method to help diabetics by transplanting insulin-producing beta cells. Stuart also pointed out that many diabetics can't afford the cost of insulin, syringes and other supplies without a private health plan. It was a comprehensive article on diabetes, clearly written out of concern for those with the illness, including, and especially, Ina.

Ina was living in her parents' home at the time. But after she had dated Stuart for a few months, she moved out. An acquaintance had left Ottawa for the summer, and suggested to Ina that she use her apartment. Ina boxed up her clothes and transported them to her new place while her parents were visiting relatives in

Montreal. When Sarah returned, Ina advised her mother that she had moved out. Needless to say, Sarah wasn't very happy about this surprise. But after she began thinking about it more, Sarah realized that Ina might need a place of her own after spending her university years away.

"I was making the meals, we were down her neck," Sarah says.

(Sarah made Ina a salad for lunch every day packed in Tupperware. Ina was famous at the *Ottawa Citizen* for her salads.)

If her daughter had to leave home, Sarah wanted her to live in a nice apartment. The two looked around at a few places, then Ina said she had changed her mind and would stay home after all.

About a year after Stuart and Ina met, Ina got the surprise of her life.

Stuart knocked on her door at 11 p.m. one Sunday night, holding flowers, a bottle of champagne and a large piece of paper. The piece of paper was a copy of the next day's front page of the *Ottawa Sun*. It was dated Monday, December 10, 1990. The page showed a smiling Stuart holding several balloons, roses, a bottle of champagne, two champagne glasses, and most importantly, a sign that said: "Ina will you marry me?" Underneath to the right was a picture of Ina, with a subhead that read: "A Love-ly Idea!"

Stuart also wrote a column for page two, headlined "Just Say Yes, Ina."

"Whatever you do Ina, just say yes. Yes to what? Well,

Ina Sue Swedler, will you please marry me? Just so you know, dear readers, it isn't easy sending out 43,000-odd proposals to the gal I love. As to why I'd do it in the *Sun*, well…First, we're both journalists, me here at the *Sun* and Ina over at the competition, the *Ottawa Citizen*. Second, we met through the newspaper. A year ago September, the girl of my dreams penned a wonderful story that caught my eye. Along with the story was a photograph of Ina and her mother Sarah at work in the kitchen…"

Stuart went on to explain how the two had met with Maria's help, then he continued, "Now let me tell you a bit about the girl I want to be my wife. She's got a great smile and a dynamite sense of humour. Many folks will attest she'd done wonders to curb my horrible temper and as of 11 days ago, Ina was the big reason I quit smoking. She also put me on a diet, started me exercising again and has generally become everything in my life. Her mom and dad, Sarah and Arnie, have almost become surrogate parents for me, insisting I show up for dinners and helping ease the gap between me here in Ottawa, and my parents, Mervyn and Estelle, back home just north of Toronto. Dad, get your tux pressed. Mom, start the cooking and baking—it's going to be another busy year. Now it's up to you Ina—just say one simple word: Yes."

The next day, the headline read, "She Said Yes!"

The follow-up article gave the details. "*Sun* reporter Stuart McCarthy and Ina Swedler celebrate after announcing their engagement yesterday. McCarthy posed on the *Sun's* front page Monday, for a surprise proposal. When Swedler saw the paper…'she screamed,' McCarthy said, adding that she also managed to scream 'yes!' Congrats you two."

Stuart and Ina were married by Rabbi Bulka at the Machzikei Hadas synagogue. Ina tripped on the stairs just before reaching the aisle, and the congregation gasped. But she righted herself quickly and laughed, then marched down the aisle with her mother at her right and her father at her left. This was a joyful occasion, one that Arnie lists as a favorite memory.

Arnie's speech was outstanding, Sarah remembers. Arnie called Ina up to the podium and told her how wonderful she was, how proud he was of her, how she never gave him any trouble. His voice cracked. There were tears in his eyes. He joked that now that both his children were married, he and Sarah should try to have another child. Everyone laughed. What made the wedding even more special for Arnie was that it took place on Father's Day.

Ina forbid the caterer—a friend of Arnie's—to serve chicken with the leg sticking up at her wedding. Chicken breast was alright. The leg sticking up wasn't. If there was a chicken that had a leg sticking up, Ina was leaving the premises. This is something the Swedlers still laugh about.

After the wedding ceremony and the meal, Ina donned a pair of white sneakers and danced the night away. Ina and Stuart honeymooned in Jamaica, and returned to their new home in the Hunt Club area, in the region of Ottawa South near her parents. Sarah was happy about the marriage, but also worried.

"I was worried that she was going to be out on her own and I wouldn't have the control over it, not that I had control," Sarah says.

Sarah and Ina maintained their close relationship after Ina was married. They joined each other for lunch once a week, and saw each other every Friday night, unless one was away or invited elsewhere for Shabbat dinner. Sarah and Ina also shopped together. And then, after Josh was born, Sarah became a dedicated babysitter, looking after Josh in the mornings at Ina and Stuart's home while the couple worked.

When she was only 22 and single, Ina was advised by a doctor that if she wanted to have children she should have them soon, because it would be difficult for her later. Ina, shocked, revealed this advice to her mother.

"What kind of crazy doctor is this?" Ina asked Sarah, "She told me to have babies!"

But that doctor's warnings were real.

By the time Stuart and Ina decided to have a baby, Ina's kidneys were already damaged by diabetes. The couple began the adoption process, filling out the papers and visiting a social worker. Sarah was pleased with this decision, for it meant she wouldn't have to worry about the dangers a pregnancy would pose. But then Ina and Stuart changed their minds. They decided to try to have a baby.

"Ina was a risk-taker," says Dr. Erin Keely, an endocrinologist at the Ottawa General Hospital who managed Ina's pregnancy.

Sarah believes Ina became absolutely determined to have a child during a visit to New York, when Stuart and Ina were spending the High Holidays with Harley and his wife Jane and their son Jared, who was five months old then. Ina found Jared adorable.

"Ina always loved children, being involved with children," Sarah says, remembering her daughter's days as a camp counselor. "They swarmed around her."

Harley, with dual citizenship, had moved to New York to work for an architectural firm. He married Jane Bassoon, the sister of the wife of his first cousin Jeff. To Ina, Jane was like an older sister.

Jane, a doctor specializing in adolescent medicine, says Ina had an amazing view of life; she never took herself too seriously. The morning of Ina's wedding, for example, Ina realized she had no earrings, peered at Jane's earlobes and said, "Those are nice. I'll take those." And she did. During their visits together, Jane and Ina talked endlessly, analyzing the behavioral characteristics of men, shopping (Ina loved finding 'bargoons' in the street stalls) and trying to spot famous people, having no luck.

Jane believes Ina's coping mechanism with regard to her diabetes was one of denial. Ina refused to take blood pressure medications when she needed them, Jane remembers.

"She never really thought of herself as being mortal," Jane says, "She let my mother-in-law do all the worrying so she could get on with her life. It worked for both of them. It was easier to deal with her mother than with her diabetes directly."

During her pregnancy, Ina took care of her diabetes like never before. She tested four times a day. She gave herself insulin four times a day, rather than just two. Her hemoglobin A1c, a blood test which measures diabetic control over three previous months, was perfect. For the first time in her life, Ina enjoyed stellar diabetic control. And at her parents' insistence, she quit her job at the *Ottawa Sun*, as the job was too demanding for a high-risk pregnancy. She worked at her father's business to keep busy. Ina had never imagined herself toiling away at Arnie's Food Services, but it was a good option for her.

"I worried right through the pregnancy, what can I tell you?" Sarah says.

Arnie's Food Services is located in Ottawa's east end. The warehouse is stacked with canned and boxed food—canned pumpkin and tomatoes and table crackers—and there are several refrigerated rooms, full of chickens and zucchinis and cabbages and other meats and vegetables. Mostly, Arnie delivers food to local Chinese restaurants. Offices take up the second floor, with windows overlooking the warehouse. Ina worked in her father's office several hours a day, usually arriving at about 11 a.m. to take orders over the phone. Her father tickled her feet when he had a moment.

"My baby's having a baby," Arnie would say.

Ina's first cousin, David Zaltzman (Jeff's brother) was also working at Arnie's then, and he and Ina spent most of their working hours laughing. They couldn't believe how old-fashioned the warehouse was. For one thing,

Arnie has a photographic memory and can keep count of the stock in his head, so the office isn't computerized. Then there were the old-fashioned money practices. Arnie manages a bit of cash business every day and keeps the money in a cigar box. Ina saw the cigar box filled with twenty dollar bills, and she couldn't believe it. The cigar box was a running joke between David and Ina. Ina threatened to write an article about her father's business, which she didn't do, and she tried her best to try to bring her father into the twentieth century, by writing out a price list, for example.

Even with her good diabetic control and more relaxed lifestyle, Ina experienced her share of problems during the pregnancy. Her blood pressure soared. Her feet swelled so much she couldn't fit into her shoes. (She wore her mother's Reeboks—Ina was a size 6 and Sarah was a size 7.) Her legs and face ballooned also. She was losing more protein in her urine. It was clear her kidneys were worsening.

Dr. Keely admitted Ina to hospital seven weeks before the due date to watch her more carefully. It was better to wait a little longer before delivery, for the baby's sake, as long as Ina could bear it. This was a difficult time for Ina, yet she never failed to take an interest in her doctor's welfare. Whenever Dr. Keely checked up on her, Ina would ask, "How are you?" and was genuinely interested in the answer. That was Ina's personality, and Dr. Keely still marvels at the generous-mindedness of her former patient.

After 10 days in hospital, Ina could wait no longer.

Swelling, high blood pressure and kidney problems continued to plague her, so she was prepped for a Caesarean section. Nurses tried 14 times to slide an intravenous line into her veins.

"The nurses were crying," Sarah remembers. "They were so upset. Ina just took it."

Finally an anesthetist on-call was phoned, a resident named Dr. Bevan Bart. Thankfully, he was successful in getting the needle in right away.

Josh sailed through. He was born small (four pounds, four ounces) but healthy. He was kept in the neonatal intensive care unit for observation for a day, then moved to the regular nursery. After six days, Ina was discharged from hospital, but Josh needed to stay there because he was too small to go home.

That was hard for Stuart and Ina, leaving Josh in the hospital when they returned home. For the next six weeks, Ina came back to the hospital every day to breast-feed her son, cuddle him, whisper to him. She pumped her breasts and filled hospital fridges with her breast milk so the nurses could feed Josh at night.

Ina had taken a risk, and it had paid off. She and Stuart had a beautiful, healthy son.

This was the best of times for Sarah. When she speaks of Josh's birth, Sarah glows with pride. And she laughs, especially about Dr. Bart and the salami incident.

Dr. Bart helped put the Swedlers at ease during and immediately after the delivery. He and Arnie chatted about Arnie's business at one point, so a few weeks after Josh was born, when Josh was still in the nursery, the

Swedlers decided to give Dr. Bart a gift. Arnie, Sarah and Ina entered the hospital bearing this gift and searched for their favorite anesthetist. They were told he was in the operating room, so they waited for him outside. When he came out in his greens, they presented him with a foot-long salami.

"I can't believe this. Only us," Ina commented to her mother.

When she returned home, Ina phoned Harley immediately to tell him about the salami. Ina, of course, loved a good story.

No family could be closer. Harley and Ina clearly adored each other. He was her big brother, her mentor, her friend, who always included her in his plans with his buddies. And Ina and Arnie were alike in so many ways. Both kept their feelings inside, didn't complain about their troubles, and shared the attitude that everything would turn out fine. Ina also had a lot of Sarah in her— her tenacity, her caring attitude toward others, her love of motherhood.

Ina read to Josh constantly. She taught him the alphabet. She and Stuart took him to see the fireworks on Parliament Hill on Canada Day when he was only three months old. She tended to keep him up late at night to spend more time with him, as if she knew their time together would not be long.

Ina's kidneys continued to decline after the pregnancy. This was likely inevitable, regardless of whether Ina had become pregnant or not.

Explains Caroline Bassoon, an endocrinologist who

also practices high-risk obstetrics and is married to Ina's first cousin Jeff, "Ina had kidney disease before the pregnancy. At some point in her lifetime she would have ended up on dialysis needing a transplant. But maybe it wouldn't have happened a year after Josh was born. It may have happened three years after Josh was born. It may have changed the duration of time leading to end-stage kidney disease but it doesn't change the outcome that much. But no one even knows that, because she had high enough protein even before she became pregnant, that it would have been possible that she would have ended up in the same stage at the same time, even if the pregnancy didn't take place."

Ina never, ever regretted having Josh. In fact, Stuart and Ina often talked of having another baby, a sister or brother for Josh. Ina once told Jennifer O'Malley, her old roommate from the McGill days: "I would never do anything different. Having Josh was the best thing I ever did."

Ina and Harley in
Florida.

Planting trees in Israel.

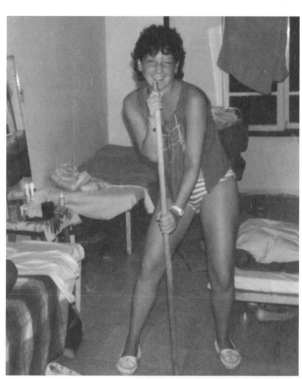

Ina overseas, "touring" Europe.

Ina and Sarah rollerblading in South Beach, Florida, 1990.

Valentine's Day 1990 in Florida.

Ina's wedding day, June 16, 1991. The radiant bride with her matron of honor and sister-in-law Jane Swedler (left) and flower girl Alina Zaltzman.

Ina at work at the *Ottawa Sun*.

Ina as bridesmaid for her friend Donna, 1995.

CHAPTER 7

Worse Off Than Me

Ina began dialysis in the summer of 1995. This was Sarah's fear come true, the one she had carried with her since she first learned about dialysis all those years ago, when Ina was just a child.

"I think," Sarah says now, "I slowly died when Ina went on dialysis."

Ina had the choice of hemodialysis in the hospital or peritoneal dialysis at home. She chose peritoneal dialysis, because to her it meant more freedom. Hemodialysis requires spending several hours in the hospital three times a week. The hemodialysis machine rids the blood of toxins that accumulate in the body because the kidneys can no longer do the job. Peritoneal dialysis is just as effective at this as hemodialysis, but it works in a different way. Four times a day, patients empty a bagful of fluid from their abdomen and replace it with clean fluid that comes in a bag. The exchange, which patients do on their own, takes about 20 minutes. People on peritoneal dialysis need a permanent tube called a catheter implanted into their bellies. They also need two weeks of training at a hospital.

Just before her catheter surgery, Ina phoned her friend Faye Goldman from the hospital. (Incidentally, Faye married Michael, Ina's ex-boyfriend who gave her the Inuit sculpture for her Sweet 16.) Faye asked Ina how she felt about the surgery.

Ina replied that she felt OK, adding matter-of-factly: "There are a lot of people worse off than me."

Faye won't soon forget that comment. Neither will Sarah, who overheard it and thinks about it whenever she is feeling down.

Dialysis improved Ina's health immediately. She had more energy, her colour was brighter. And dialysis did not stop Ina from living her life. She continued to work at the *Ottawa Business Journal*, often broadcasting the CFRA daily business report from home. She took Josh tobogganing, climbing on the sled alongside him. She enrolled Josh in a swimming class at night, and joined him in the pool. (People on peritoneal dialysis are not allowed to swim in lakes, but can swim in pools and oceans, because chlorine and salt prevent infections from the water at the site of the catheter.) One day, when the temperature was -40 degrees Celsius, Ina ventured out to a field to go cross-country skiing by herself, and her car was broken into, a window was smashed and her purse was stolen. Sarah was livid when she heard about this.

She said, "Ina, if not for me, then for your son, how could you possibly go alone, diabetic, you're on dialysis, without a phone, and these people that broke into your car could have come after you, and God knows what they would have done."

Sarah was continually shocked by her daughter's dogged fight to maintain a life that was vital, by her daughter's risk-taking, and by her seeming nonchalance toward the disease that was gnawing away at her body. Even before Ina went on dialysis, it was clear that her kidneys would give out eventually. The creatinine level in her blood, a measurement of kidney function, was rising. There were increasing amounts of protein in her urine, another bad sign. In fact, six months before she needed dialysis, Ina exited her doctor's office with a question that caught Sarah by surprise.

"Mom, how are your kidneys?" Ina asked casually. "I might need one."

She asked it as though she was asking to borrow five dollars, Sarah remembers. At the time, Ina was being followed at the Ottawa General Hospital by a nephrologist named Dr. David Levine, because Dr. Keely was away on leave. This was the first mention of transplant for Ina, at the end of 1994 when Josh was eight months old. There was no immediacy for a kidney transplant, but planning for it was important, because a match needed to be found. There was still time. Dialysis would, and did, put off the inevitable for awhile.

Even on dialysis, Ina was able to work for the local Hadassah organization, a Jewish women's fundraising group. She was the membership co-chair, recruiting and welcoming new members. Tired and hooked up to a machine, she processed all the membership information. "She never said, 'I can't do this,'" says Jackie Barwin, a friend.

At the end of 1995, Ina and Stuart decided to go to Cuba together for a week. As sick as Ina was, she and Stuart packed up the dialysis machine and numerous boxes of bags of dialysis fluid and boarded a plane for the beaches of Cuba. Stuart phoned Cuban authorities for permission to take the equipment.

Soon after the Cuba trip, Harley, Sarah, Arnie and Stuart were tested to see if their kidneys matched. Arnie wasn't considered, because he had high blood pressure and therefore needed both his kidneys. The human body regards anything foreign as hostile and something to attack, so a good match is important. It means less chance of rejecting the donor organ. Incredibly, Sarah, Harley and Stuart were all good matches. Given there were three who matched, it didn't seem wise for Stuart to give his kidney, because he needed to stay healthy for Josh. That left Harley and Sarah. Each went through a battery of tests—blood tests, urine tests, a physical—to see if they were healthy enough to donate. Harley had these tests done in New York; Sarah had them performed in Ottawa. They both needed blood typing, tissue typing, screening for viruses such as hepatitis and HIV, routine blood work, 24-hour urine collections, a chest X-ray, an ultrasound of the abdomen, a renal arteriogram and psychological assessment. Harley argued with Sarah, because he wanted to be the one to donate the kidney. But it made more sense for Sarah to be the donor. Harley had a young family to care for—Jared, who was four and Marlee, who was a baby then. As well, if Harley donated his kidney, and it failed after a while, then Ina would have to turn to Sarah, and Sarah might be too old for the surgery at that point. For these reasons, the family finally agreed that Sarah was the most reasonable choice. She was still healthy. And like Harley, she would cherish the chance to do something so significant for her daughter. Says Heidi Lemish, Ina's first cousin: "My aunt would have given all her kidneys."

Sarah and Ina shared a joke about the kidney transplant. They imagined themselves in adjacent operating rooms. Ina has just received Sarah's kidney, and it won't work. She can't pee. And Sarah can hear Ina screaming from the next room, "Mom, your kidney's not working!"

"Everything was my fault in life," Sarah now sighs, with a sly smile.

Sarah had two tests left to do. One was the renal arteriogram, a kidney X-ray using a special dye, done to ensure her kidney functioned properly. The other was psychological testing, necessary to check on whether Sarah could handle the stresses of a transplant. But she never had these tests done, because Ina changed her mind. Ina wouldn't, couldn't take her mother's kidney. Ina broke the news to her mother while they were visiting the hospital for some reason. She said she'd get a cadaver kidney instead.

Sarah couldn't believe it. "I was devastated. I was so upset. I couldn't talk her out of it," she says.

Crying, Sarah ran to the transplant co-ordinator at the General, a woman named Suzanne. Suzanne offered Sarah some statistics that were of some comfort. A cadaver kidney had a 85 per cent success rate, compared to a 95 per cent success rate for a kidney from a living relative—a difference of only 10 per cent. Suzanne wrote the numbers down for Sarah on a piece of yellow paper that Sarah has kept to this day. She also told Sarah that, ultimately, it was Ina's choice. Sarah sometimes blames herself for being unable to convince Ina to take her kidney. At times, she thinks she didn't push hard enough because she was afraid of having her kidney removed. But Sarah did push, and she knew Ina well enough to know when to give up.

Why wouldn't Ina take her mother's kidney? Was she afraid something terrible would happen to her mother? Did she want to go through her trials alone, without involving anyone else? Was she afraid her mother would never forgive herself if the transplant failed? For whatever reason, Ina refused to take the gift of her mother's kidney. Others would have taken it without thinking, but for Ina, diabetes was a challenge she chose to face on her own terms.

There's a more disturbing question than why Ina refused Sarah's kidney. And it's this: Would things have turned out differently if she had taken it?

The wait for a cadaver kidney in Ottawa was about a month. Just when Sarah had accepted the notion of a cadaver kidney, before Ina was even put on the waiting list, Ina changed her mind again. She had heard about another option, an option she thought would rid her of diabetes forever.

The answer lay in a kidney-pancreas transplant.

She had heard about the experimental treatment

through the owner of the *Ottawa Business Journal,* whose sister-in-law Barbra Ikeman had recently received the first pancreas transplant in Canada. The idea of a pancreas transplant appealed to Ina, and she began to research the option. Thousands of pancreas transplants had been done worldwide, especially in the United States. The pancreas contains beta cells, which produce insulin. In diabetics, for reasons that aren't well-understood, the patient's own immune system attacks these islets. Replacing the pancreas fixes the problem, restoring normal insulin-producing islets to the body. The first successful pancreas transplant was done in 1966 by surgeons in Minnesota. The Toronto Hospital began its program in the mid-1990s. (Islets alone have also been transplanted, but whole pancreas transplants have generally been found to be more successful.)

For Ina, a new pancreas represented freedom from diabetes. No more insulin. No more needles. And since a kidney is often transplanted simultaneously with the pancreas, Ina would no longer need dialysis either. However, she would need to take immunosuppressant drugs for the rest of her life, so that the new organs wouldn't be rejected.

There are bonuses to a pancreas transplant. It can prevent diabetes-associated problems from recurring in the donated kidney, since blood sugar is well-controlled. It can also improve the nerve and blood vessel problems connected to diabetes, and researchers have found that most patients believe their quality of life is better after the operation than before.

Ina weighed the options and decided to risk the operation. The worst that could happen, she believed, was rejection of the new organs and a return to dialysis or insulin. What she wanted, more than anything, was to be well again after 20 years of sickness, to be like everyone else.

Ina took the train to Toronto in February 1996 to meet her potential surgeon, as well as other medical staff, at Toronto Hospital. One of the first questions Ina asked was whether she could have another child after the procedure. The answer was yes, that it was possible after a year. A drawback of the surgery was having to stay for two months in Toronto afterward. Sarah remembers a piece of advice Ina received from one of the doctors at the Toronto Hospital. A kidney specialist warned her not to choose the pancreas transplant, explaining she should take advantage of her two matching living kidney donors. "She didn't want to hear it," Sarah says.

Ina turned 30 years old that year. She was looking forward to this landmark so much, that Stuart and Sarah threw her a surprise party at Sarah's new home upon Ina's return from Toronto. Sarah rented tables for the affair. Ina was truly surprised; she arrived wearing a Mickey Mouse sweatshirt. Stuart, however, had brought her a change of clothes. It was a huge party, a celebration of Ina's triumphs in the face of so many challenges.

Her pre-surgery testing was done in Ottawa. Ina had blood tests; she saw her eye doctor; she visited the dentist; she had her heart tested. Her heart was examined with an echocardiogram and electrocardiogram. Ina received her beeper in the spring, hoping to get called for the pancreas transplant within four to six weeks. She expected the beep at any moment. But it took longer than a month to get beeped. It took five months. May and June went OK. The Swedlers spent Passover in New York with Harley and Jane and their kids. Harley and Jane held two seders.

"I have a picture of Ina," muses Sarah. "She was beautiful, glowing. She really did look beautiful."

One day during this visit the extended Swedler family trekked to the circus at Madison Square Garden. The kids all wore sweaters decorated with the American flag, provided by Sarah. It was a good time, a memorable one. After the circus they found a diner that served kosher-for-Passover food. The family was excited to find such a restaurant in a non-Jewish area. They ate matzah ball soup.

July and August went badly, however. Ina's stomach began to bloat from fluid retention, a result of the dialysis. At one point she looked nine months pregnant. An infection was suspected, but never proven. Ina also had an umbilical hernia, in which her bellybutton poked out inches, and she had to wear a brace to keep it tucked in. Whenever Sarah visited Ina, the sight of the dialysis machine made her "truthfully sick."

Says Sarah, "I tried not to learn too much about dialysis. Diabetes I could tell you everything, but not dialysis."

Sarah decided to have a family picture done during the July 4th weekend, when Harley and Jane and their children were in town. "My heart told me," she says.

A bit of good news came from the producers of the Discovery Channel. They wanted to film a pancreas transplant for a medical show, and Ina was up for the part. The idea was to film Ina before, during and after the operation. They planned to film Ina performing home dialysis, taking care of Josh, and basically follow her around for a couple of days before the operation. Ina thought this was great; she had always wanted to be an actress. She loved stardom. In fact, Harley used to tease her with his anecdotes of star-sightings in New York City. He would brag about walking past John F. Kennedy Jr. on the street, and this used to drive Ina crazy. In New York, Ina never seemed to run into a star. "Everybody sees a star but me," she would moan. The show she loved most was *Regis and Kathie Lee*. And when Charles Gibson came to Ottawa and Hull to broadcast his morning show at the Museum of Civilization, Ina managed to snag a guest pass. She had the opportunity to talk to Gibson, and told him about her future pancreas transplant and did he think that would make an interesting topic on the show? Unfortunately, he wasn't interested.

So Ina looked forward to her role on the Discovery Channel. True, it wasn't *Regis and Kathie Lee*, but nevertheless it was show business. Ina joked to her boss Mark Sutcliffe that her kidneys would be more famous than she was. She joked to her mother that the surgeons wouldn't want to make any mistakes while the film was rolling.

But the filming never took place. On their way to

Ottawa from somewhere in the States, the crew members were called and were told another person they had considered for the show had just been beeped for the transplant. The crew turned around. They never made it to Ottawa. Ina took this hard. It was a disappointment, and it happened about the same time her health took a downturn.

She was becoming increasingly agitated, short-tempered, fed-up. Sarah was concerned. Ina was too thin, her coloring had returned to its yellow hue. Friends of Sarah would comment on how great Ina looked, how thin she had become, but Sarah knew better. "I thought if something isn't done, I see her deteriorating right in front of my eyes. You know when you see somebody fading, that's how I felt. I knew this wait was too long."

Sarah tried to convince Ina to switch to hemodialysis in the hospital and Ina considered it. The fact was, Ina was sick of hospitals. And she felt spending so many hours in hospital would take her away from Josh. In any case, Ina was starting to rethink her dialysis strategy. Sarah also tried to convince her daughter to change the location of her operation to New York City, where more pancreas transplants were being done than in Toronto, and where she had family to help out, including Jane. Ina would consider this if the wait was much longer. Ina suggested going to Las Vegas with her mother for a weekend, because she wanted to get out of town. But Sarah didn't think it was wise to stray too far from home while Ina was waiting to be beeped. Ina frequently checked in with the transplant co-ordinator at the

Toronto Hospital, and was always told she was still on the list and it was just a matter of when.

One day Ina met her mother at the Hard Rock Cafe in Ottawa for lunch. Sarah was sitting at the window waiting for her, and when she saw her: "my heart, I was crying, I just looked at her and I thought, what has happened to this gorgeous smiling…she walked in and said hi, mom, sorry to keep you waiting, she was really looking bad."

Shortly afterward, after Sarah spent a sleepless night worrying, she drove to the Ottawa General Hospital at 6 a.m., waiting for Ina's home dialysis nurse—the nurse who had taught Ina how to exchange the fluid and who monitored her regularly. When the nurse came into the hospital for work, she had to see a patient first, and then she tried to calm Sarah. She explained that Ina was undergoing a lot of stress after moving into a new home in the Ottawa suburb of Barrhaven (Farrhaven, to Sarah). Moving was stressful, not to mention the wait for the transplant. Sarah returned home, still worried.

But then, the worries ended, because Ina finally did get beeped.

We always shopped together. I used to say in front of the salespeople. Ina, buy it, buy. They used to say, the salespeople, can you please adopt me. I got such pleasure out of shopping with her, especially when she tried on something that really looked funny on her we would burst into laughter. She was so appreciative of it and sometimes got very angry at me. I would always say, Dad and I get such pleasure out of doing all the things for you now than after we're gone. I can barely go shopping for myself now as the first thing I look for is things that Ina would like.

Sarah Swedler, notes.

CHAPTER 8

The Operation

The call came on Saturday, September 20, two days before Yom Kippur, the holiest of Jewish holidays. Sarah slipped into a pair of jeans and drove up to Ina's house to help her pack.

"Ina, are you nervous?" Sarah asked.

"Slightly, mom."

Josh's nanny Edith came to take care of Josh, while Stuart and Ina took off to the airport in a taxi. Ina phoned Mark Sutcliffe from the taxi to tell him the good news. "So piss off and leave me alone for a few months," she laughed.

Meanwhile, a couple of Sarah's friends came over to help Sarah pack for her stay in Toronto. She planned to live at the Delta Inn for about a week after Ina's surgery, then rent an apartment for herself and Ina near the Toronto Hospital after Ina was discharged. The idea was for Ina to stay close to the hospital for two months in case she had a problem, a requirement of the pancreas transplant program. A few days after the operation, Edith would bring Josh to Toronto, and Josh would stay in the Toronto apartment with Ina and Edith, attending the nursery school at George Brown College. Stuart would join his wife and son on weekends. (Sarah planned to stay with relatives on weekends to give the couple privacy.)

It was suggested, at first, that Sarah and Arnie stay in Ottawa with Josh during the actual operation, then drive to Toronto later. Sarah refused that role. She couldn't believe it was even suggested, explaining sarcastically, "My daughter was having an operation, then Arnie and I would slowly drive to Toronto! I told Ina, Ina you know darn well, even if a mother wasn't devoted, she'd have to be insane to think that she would stay behind, and you would have to be more insane to think that I would be capable of even looking at Josh. Be glad if I'd be able to stand up. I said, I'm going to Toronto the minute you're beeped."

She and Arnie flew into Toronto and arrived just after Ina had been taken into the operating room. Harley and Jane were already there, and of course Stuart, as well as the McCarthys. Jeff, Ina's first cousin who also happened to be a kidney transplant specialist at St. Mike's Hospital, was there with his wife Caroline. Caroline, an endocrinologist, is Jane's sister. Jane is a family doctor specializing in adolescent medicine. Ina's sister-in-law Frances is a dialysis nurse and Frances' husband Harold is a doctor of internal medicine. Ina's first cousin Susan Brinker is an intensive care nurse at Mount Sinai Hospital, across the street from the Toronto Hospital. It seemed like everyone waiting outside the operating room had either a medical or nursing degree.

The operation lasted eight hours, from 1 p.m. to 9 p.m. (Surgeons fixed the umbilical hernia at the same time as the two transplants.) At one point during the long wait, Jane and Sarah paced down the hallway near the operating theatres and came upon a quiet, comfortable room. They sat inside it, and after a few minutes Sarah wondered what the room was used for. Jane looked around. "I think it's the condolence room," she whispered. Sarah felt a shiver, and they both got up and left.

When the surgery had ended, Ina's surgeon Dr. Mark Cattral emerged from the operating room to report that the operation had gone well. Ina would need to stay in the intensive care unit for a bit, and they could see her there in 45 minutes. Ina had gotten her wish. She had a new kidney. She had a new pancreas. She was off insulin. Sarah thought her daughter looked good, better than expected. Ina was talking, asking her mother why a woman in the next bed was screaming. Late at night, Harley returned to the intensive care unit by himself. Ina was sleeping. He stared at her. This was his little sister. It was like she was 10 years old again. There were tubes everywhere. He wanted to sleep over at the hospital; he didn't want to leave her alone. This is a regret Harley lives with now—that he didn't sleep over that night.

The next day, the intensive care unit was deluged with so many phone calls from people inquiring about Ina that the nurses had to advise the Swedlers to designate one person who could inform family and friends. This was Sunday, the day before Yom Kippur. Back in Ottawa, Rabbi Bulka gave a special Kol Nidray sermon the night that Ina slept in the intensive care unit. He spoke about the need for transplants, and he spoke about Ina.

Sarah keeps a copy of Rabbi Bulka's Kol Nidray sermon in her scrapbook.

Her mother and her brother and her husband graciously volunteered to donate one of their kidneys to her, but Ina refused. Perhaps one of her considerations was that she did not want to put either her mother or her brother or her husband in jeopardy, lest they have difficulty with their only remaining kidney. But probably foremost in the back of her mind was the idea that if she held out, maybe at one point or another the blessing of a combined kidney-pancreas transplant would be forthcoming. Then, she could simultaneously be off insulin, and also off regular dialysis, which she has been on now for quite some time. I need not tell you that if daily insulin is an intrusion on your life, dialysis is even more pronounced and invasive. And so the family was proceeding apace, and at the same time Ina kept up to all the medical protocols that she needed to satisfy the demands that were placed on her because of her condition. And then, a few days ago came a sudden call from Toronto that yes, there was a kidney and there was a pancreas, that were both matches for Ina. She and Stuart were in Toronto on the double, and

within the space of a few hours she was on the oper-
ating table with a functioning kidney and a func-
tioning pancreas. Today was the first day in years
that she did not have to give herself an insulin injec-
tion. Thankfully she is doing well, although there is
a long road ahead. This is serious surgery, quite inva-
sive, as you can understand, and there is a long road
of potential difficulties before she is in the
clear....Now you legitimately ask me a very good
question. Rabbi, this is a very nice story, and we are
all terribly happy for Ina and her family, but what
does this have to do with Yom Kippur? And besides,
transplant is exotic surgery, it only happens rarely,
and why should this rare occurrence occupy our
attention tonight? Well, the question is a good ques-
tion and it demands a vigorous answer. We are not
here talking simply about transplantation of organs.
We are talking here about lifesaving, about our being
vigilant and attentive to the opportunities that are
around us on a regular basis, to save other peoples'
lives. Is there anything more sacred than to be con-
cerned about saving other people's lives? If there is I
would like to know...

On Sunday night, Ina was transferred to the step-
down unit, a place for patients not sick enough for intensive care but who still need to be monitored closely. Ina
had a routine ultrasound on Monday morning, and Dr.
Cattral didn't like the look of it. He asked for another
ultrasound. There was bad news. A blood clot was found

in a vein draining the new pancreas. Sarah didn't know if this was serious or not, but it made her nervous. She was the only family member in the hospital. She felt alone, and nervous. Stuart had gone back to Ottawa, starting a new job and planning to return in a few days. Arnie had to take care of his business. Harley and Jane had flown back to New York City.

Ina underwent angiography to examine the clot further. Sarah, a nurse named Louise, and Dr. Cattral pulled Ina's bed through a tunnel to get to the radiology department for the procedure. The cart bumped along the corridor. Ina almost fell out. Sarah sat alone for two hours outside the room during the angiogram. She was relieved when Stuart's father Mervyn showed up to join her. The two waited, worried, until Dr. Cattral came out and announced the blockage couldn't be cleared. (Removing the clot with a suction catheter was unsuccessful.) Afterward, Ina was put on blood-thinner medication to try to dissolve the clot away.

Flowers covered the nurses' station in the step-down unit. There were so many flowers the room resembled a florist's shop. Calls continued to come in from friends and relatives. Again, the nurses advised Sarah the calls were getting out-of-hand.

Jane called each morning at 6 a.m. Sarah called the nurses every morning too, even though she was just down the street in her hotel and would soon be in the room herself.

Susan Brinker, Ina's first cousin, checked on Ina three times a day, because she was working across the street at the Mount Sinai Hospital and could take a tunnel to the Toronto Hospital. Susan wore a green or pink nurse's uniform and managed to cheer her cousin. They spoke about how they really wanted to be actors, instead of their present occupations. Ina promised she would write a movie script and they would both star in the film.

On Tuesday night, Ina had a special visitor. It was Rabbi Bulka, holding a little plant with a pink flower in a glass vase. He was on his way by plane from New York to Ottawa with a wait at the Toronto airport, and during the wait he took a taxi to the hospital to see Ina. Rabbi Bulka felt a genuine affection for Ina. He admired her cheeriness, her friendliness and her warmth. Sarah thought the pink flower would bring Ina the best of luck. "I *believed* in those days," she now sighs.

And Ina did have good luck for several days. Wednesday was wonderful. One by one, tubes came out. The tube in her mouth, the tube in her nose, a tube in her leg. The main topic of conversation was the fact that JFK Jr. had just gotten married. Ina asked Sarah to bring her newspapers and magazines so she could read about it. "She was always crazy about him," Sarah says. "She thought he was the most gorgeous thing on this earth. She was in love with him. She said, 'imagine, he didn't wait for me.'"

Ina took a shower, felt like a human being again. Sarah blow-dried her hair, being extra-careful with the bangs because of the importance Ina placed on bangs. Ina promised Sarah that in future she would get involved in fundraising for transplants. This was a surprise to Sarah, as Ina had never become involved with diabetes fundraising.

Then Ina got her period, and managed to laugh about it. She joked that other people missed their period because of the stress of a relationship break-up, and here she couldn't even miss her period after the stress of two transplants. She also, jokingly, threatened to steal the pump that was doling out her pain medication, because for once she had no menstrual pain.

During this time, Ina was able to write a few letters, which Sarah faxed from her hotel.

Dear Stuart,

Hey it's mommy here! How are you? Did we get the Jetform deal? I'm feeling a lot better than on Monday. I had an ultrasound today and the clot is still there but better. They're going to keep watching it and another ultrasound Friday…My nose tube is out and my art line too. Also they put in my IV block for fluid (only 2 tries). How's Josh? I can't wait to see him!! Don't forget his books, toys, dog, sus!! And some of his videos! (If they don't have one at Minto we could bring one of ours from home!) Oh yah—I'd love my Gund bear too! Anyway, I hope all is well there! I can't wait to see you guys! Hopefully, I'll be in my own room tomorrow. Send a fax to mom at the hotel and she'll bring it to me!

I love you guys!!

Ina

Dear Jane and Harley,
Just a quick note to let you know I'm doing OK. Had an ultrasound today and the clot looks a bit better—they're keeping an eye on it. Nose tube and art lines are history. Other than that feeling pretty good today! Just wanted to say hi!
All my love, Ina.

Dear Mark and OBJ and gang,
Hey it's me, the lady of new organs! Just wanted to send you guys a quick note—thanks for the small garden—the flowers are beautiful. I'm feeling more chipper today—some tubes are coming out and I'm starting to feel human. Kidney is working great— pancreas too but I do have a clot in vein near the pancreas causing some concern. I'm moving into my own room tonight so I'll have access to a phone and TV. I had a glass of orange juice today—isn't life great. Had a dream I forgot to do the radio one day—yikes. My mom is faxing this from her hotel so fax back if you can! Hope all is well and paper looks good ! Miss you guys a lot!
Love, Ina.

Says Sarah: "Why I didn't bring my camera I don't know. Ina and I spoke about it, that we'd be taking pictures from the beginning. She was going to write her own story on it, maybe a book. She wanted photos." In the commotion of packing after Ina was beeped, Sarah forgot the camera.

Visitors began pouring in—Ina's first cousins Susan and her sister Diane, Sarah's sister Nettie and brother Sam from Montreal and Sam's wife Edna, a former nurse. Everyone was surprised to see how well Ina looked. She was sitting up, laughing, talking. She had walked a bit. Sam took the gang out for supper at the Barbarian Restaurant to celebrate.

Jeff remained cautious, though. He hoped for the best, of course, and he told Sarah he didn't want to frighten her, but he warned her not to become too over-joyed, as there would be ups and downs, and there was the problem of the blood clot.

Sarah began looking for an apartment, as planned. She found a beautiful, bright one in Minto Place, across the street from her hotel and close to the hospital. Sarah looked forward to spending time with Ina during the convalescence period. She planned to invite nurses and doctors to a party when Ina felt well enough. Sarah imagined her daughter gradually getting better in this beautiful apartment, off insulin, off dialysis, a new future before her.

On Thursday, Sarah brought Ina the white terry cloth robe, so that she wouldn't shiver when she walked. Stuart drove in on Thursday night with Josh and Edith. Josh sat on Ina's bed playing. Edith had gotten married two weeks before, but generously offered to spend the weekdays in Toronto with Josh and Ina, going home on weekends.

That Thursday night, Sarah put the calls on hold. There were too many, and Ina needed rest.

Ina worsened on Friday. She began to feel nauseous. She felt so badly she could barely play with Josh.

"She was nauseous, nauseous, nauseous," says Sarah. "She was throwing up bile. They were bringing food, she couldn't touch anything."

Ina tried to walk to the corner window in the corridor with her walker, but grew tired and had to lie down. Her face became a little heavier. Sarah had the phone disconnected and allowed no visitors. From then on, Sarah says she had the most sick feeling.

Saturday was no better. Ina was feeling more and more ill. Her face was truly bloated now. Arnie flew in that morning. Dr. Cattral explained to Sarah that the patient who had received the other kidney from the same donor was also having a difficult time. On Sunday night, Stuart and Arnie returned to Ottawa. While Sarah knew in her heart things were going wrong, others seemed to expect such problems as a matter of course, and felt confident. Sarah wanted to beg her husband to stay, but she knew he had to run his business. Jeff and Caroline were away on a medical conference in Halifax and would return to Toronto on Sunday.

Ina began to second-guess her decision to have the pancreas transplant. Twice she asked Sarah if she had done the right thing by going that route. Ina insisted that she never felt as bad on dialysis as she felt then. Sarah admonished her, saying, of course you did the right thing, you've been off insulin for days, and you knew there would be ups and downs. Looking back, Sarah realizes that Ina's self-doubts should have indicated very serious problems, because it was rare for Ina to wonder about her decisions.

"That should have signaled me how sick she was," Sarah says. "That should have been my yelling and screaming."

Ina's friend Melissa Greenberg visited Ina on Sunday. They talked a bit, and when it was time to leave, Melissa mouthed "I love you" to Ina. She felt like someone was telling her to say that then. Ina looked at her friend, smiled and blew her a kiss.

"I'm so happy I got to say that," Melissa says. "In a way, I felt like I was representing all her friends."

Jeff and Caroline returned to the hospital directly from the airport on Sunday night. Jeff saw a very ill patient.

Sarah recalls, "Jeffrey said, 'Get Dr. Cattral, get him on his car phone, get him at home, get him on his beeper. Get him wherever you have to get him."

Jeff thought Ina should be dialysed. "I was berserk, I was berserk," Sarah says. "Caroline had these big black eyes. I saw the terror."

A kidney specialist came by, and got Dr. Cattral on the phone. They would dialyse Ina the next day.

"I regret I didn't sleep over. I don't know why I didn't sleep over," Sarah says.

Monday morning, Sarah rose early. The bellboy carried her luggage to the new apartment at Minto Place while Sarah ran to the hospital. Ina was sitting up in bed, laboring for breath. There was a portable X-ray machine in the room.

"Mom, you're out of focus." Ina whispered. "I can't see you. I'm so sick. I'm so sick."

Ina, who had progressed to a private room, was moved back to the step-down unit and hooked up to a heart monitor. The nurses asked Sarah to remove all the flowers from the private room, as a new patient would be coming in immediately. There were so many flowers, about 40 flowers, too many for Sarah to handle alone. Sarah called Stuart's father Mervyn and asked him to come help her carry the flowers. Caroline would stay with Ina until it was time for her dialysis. Sarah found an empty food cart in the hallway. Two trips would be needed to carry all the flowers. Mervyn's car was waiting at the front door of the hospital. On the first trip, when they had almost reached the car, the cart hit a bump and Rabbi Bulka's flower smashed on the pavement. The little pink flower lay in a clump of soil amid the glass. And when Sarah saw this, she had a horrible realization that her daughter might not live.

When Sarah and Mervyn returned to Ina, the staff asked them to leave the room while Ina was being dialysed. Mervyn left the hospital, while Caroline and Sarah went downstairs to the cafeteria, a dingy room in the basement.

It was ten minutes past four when they came back upstairs to the step-down unit. The door was closed. Caroline glanced at her watch. The unit's rest period was between 2 and 4 p.m., so it was strange for the door to be closed.

"We're going in," Caroline said.

Two doctors hovered around Ina. They said they hadn't dialysed her because they couldn't find a vein. They tried on one arm, then the other, and they simply couldn't get the needle in.

Caroline said out loud, "She looks very pale."

Then the door suddenly opened and about ten doctors and nurses rushed in.

"I'm going to faint," Sarah said.

"Please Auntie Sarah, go downstairs," Caroline said. And Sarah said, "I can't stay here, I'm going to faint. Something is seriously, seriously wrong with Ina."

Sarah doesn't remember how she made it to the elevator. She paced in the lobby. Ina's friend Donna entered the lobby and spotted Sarah. Donna was so alarmed by what Sarah told her that she left the lobby crying and Sarah doesn't know where she went afterward. Sarah phoned Arnie and told him to get in touch with Stuart and get on the fastest plane, as Ina was very, very sick. Then Liz Wright, the transplant co-ordinator, found Sarah in the lobby and informed her that Ina's blood pressure had dropped, but the doctors were able to get it back up. "Why are they making such a fuss?" Ina had asked Liz Wright. "I feel fine now." Because the doctors didn't understand why Ina's blood pressure had plunged, they moved her into intensive care for observation.

Caroline fetched Sarah from the lobby and took her back upstairs to a room where they could wait. By now, it was about 5 or 5:30 p.m. Sarah sat on a couch and looked around. The room seemed familiar. Then she realized which room this was. It was the condolence room, the same room she had sat in during Ina's operation ten days before. Sarah closed her eyes, tried to calm herself, and heard Liz Wright being paged on the intercom. She heard her being paged again, and she knew she was being paged because of Ina. Caroline assured her there were other transplant patients, but Sarah could see the terror in Caroline's eyes.

It wasn't long before the door to the room opened and Liz Wright entered. She asked to speak to Caroline alone, and again Sarah saw the horror in Caroline's eyes. Caroline was crying now, barely able to get her words out. Ina was in cardiac arrest, but they were doing everything they could. The next thing Sarah knew, the door opened and in walked Jeff, who had been called over from St. Mike's when Ina went into cardiac arrest, and Dr. Cattral and another doctor, the head of the intensive care unit probably. And when Sarah saw them walking into the room, she knew that Ina was dead.

The rest was a blur to Sarah. Harley flew in, entered the condolence room, and the first thing he said to Sarah was, "Mom, you always knew how sick she was."

Someone handed Sarah a pill. Sarah could hear Arnie screaming in the hallway, "No, no, no, Ina, Ina…" Stuart was crying and screaming also, Sarah remembers. Every time the door opened, Sarah would hear howling from the hallway. Finally Sarah asked Harley to get her out of there. Harley made all the flight arrangements. He drove his sister in her coffin back to Ottawa. No one understood why Ina had passed away.

It made no sense for Ina to have died.

Ina's Way

AM had an eye Dr. appt. at Ottawa General. My heart was pounding as I drove up and thought of how many times Ina had suffered in pain and of course the only good time was when she had Josh. So many memories. I decided to go to the Dialysis Unit and say hi to Cheryl her nurse that taught her how to do home dialysis and always said Ina was her best patient. When I got there some of the nurses recognized me and I could see tears in their eyes also Dr. Page came over to me and asked how I was doing. I said so-so. He said I want you to know that very seldom does a person like Ina come into my life she was so special and I feel the loss terrible—and turned and said please take care Mrs. Swedler. I then went to see Susan the transplant coordinator who I went through the tests as the living donor, then how I cried in her office when Ina refused...we both cried, she also thanked me so much for stopping by and we hugged and she also said take care and come visit.

Sarah, notes written on a napkin, March 1998.

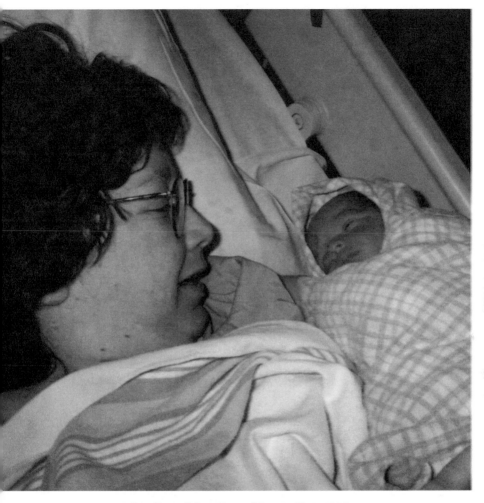

Welcoming Josh into the world on April 23, 1994.

Ina with two-year-old Josh.

**Ina's surprise party to celebrate her 30th birthday, February 23, 1996.
From left, Sarah, Jane and Ina.**

Last family photo, taken August 1996.
PHOTO: devries-mikkelsen

Josh in 1999, 5 years old.

The Diabetes Research Foundation
La Fondation de la recherche sur le diabète

Sarah with her family at the first annual ladies nine-hole golf tournament, held in Ina's memory to raise funds for the Juvenile Diabetes Foundation (Canada). From left, Arnie, Harley, Sarah, brother Sam, sister Nettie, sister-in-law Edna, and brother-in-law Harry.

CHAPTER 9

To the Full

The Swedlers no longer remember what it is like to feel pure joy. They feel a void every moment of every day. They would have rather died a thousand times than to bury their only daughter.

But then there is Josh—his smile, and his laughter, and his radiance. Ina lives on in him. He is five years old now, an intelligent, happy boy. After Ina died, Sarah needed all her strength to take her grandson to Tiny Treasures school on Friday mornings while Stuart was working. Ina had signed Josh up for the program before her operation. Watching all the other young mothers was difficult for Sarah. "What am I doing here?" Sarah would say. "Ina should be here with Josh." But these women were so kind to Sarah, crying with her, laughing with her, that Sarah invited them to her home for dinner one night. The director of the school, Devora Caytak, was also so understanding, making a point to welcome not only the mothers, but also the bubbies to the class each week. The Swedlers have become close friends with Devora and her husband Dr. Joseph Caytak, and their family, often visiting each other at holidays.

Sarah helped raise money for the school's library, even when she was trying to cope with her grief. Devora calls Sarah a person who "creates light in darkness," "a strong person," "an inspiration." Sarah looks up to Devora and appreciates her guidance.

Friday night shabbat dinners are the most painful for Sarah, because she and Arnie usually spent those evenings with Ina and Stuart and Josh, at one home or the other. "It was just a nightmare for me, to see Stuart walk up with Josh and without Ina, can you imagine the nightmare? And I did it. And I'd leave every dish after, as it was on the table. I wouldn't clean anything because I was just so drained that I'd go to bed, thinking how I'd see the empty chair and it would just be enough to..."

The Swedlers no longer have the energy to question what went wrong in that Toronto hospital that September day. Did the dye used in the angiogram damage Ina's kidney, as can sometimes occur? Should she have been placed on dialysis sooner? Was there some underlying heart problem that went unrecognized? Was her health too compromised by the time she had the operation because of the long wait? No one really knows. And does it really matter anymore? For religious reasons, only a partial autopsy was requested. Sarah spoke with Dr. Cattral at a conference in Ottawa for Organ Awareness Week more than two years after Ina died. Sarah says he told her that to this day, he doesn't know what happened after Ina's operation and that he thinks about it every day and he can't get it out of his mind. She says he added that he appreciates all the work she has done for her many causes.

Sarah and Arnie passed the Toronto Hospital in a cab recently, on the way to a wedding, and Sarah thought she might faint. She sees a psychiatrist every other week. She wants others to know this because she believes people should get help when they need it. She seems so energetic, so normal, but that isn't how she feels. Her grief is so deep that she cannot escape it.

Sarah doesn't bring flowers to Ina's grave.

"For what?" she asks. "What does it do?"

Sarah doesn't believe anymore that the hereafter exists. In any case, she always believed in doing when you're alive. She grew up thinking that if you do good things, God will reward you. She now thinks that's naive. She used to love the night before Yom Kippur, Kol Nidray, hearing on that night the beautiful voice of the cantor. Now at Yom Kippur, she mourns three generations of women. Her mother Zelda. Her sister Annie. Her daughter Ina. Three generations is too many to mourn, and the voice of the cantor no longer moves her as it once did. "God," she says, "is either blind or can't hear." She wonders if He's getting old.

Sometimes she thinks about lying on top of the ground where Ina is buried. Her biggest regret is that Ina did not take her kidney. Her greatest satisfaction involves doing things to keep Ina's memory alive.

Sarah has washed Ina's teddy bears and given about 50 of them away, to the children of Ina's friends, to Ina's little cousins.

Sarah has organized an annual golf tournament in Ina's name at the Rideau View Country Club, aided by the Nine Hole Ladies League. The tournament, which includes an afternoon of golf, a dinner and a silent auction, has raised $40,000 in the past two years for the Juvenile Diabetes Foundation. The silent auction proceeds have paid for a new room at the Children's Hospital of Eastern Ontario. It's an educational room, where doctors and nurses can teach children just diagnosed with diabetes and their parents about managing the disease. The room looks more like someone's homey kitchen than a hospital room. There's a television, and a VCR, a wooden table and wooden chairs, walls painted yellow with a mural of a garden and a gate, with a sign that reads, Ina's Way. The decorator, Donna Correy of KISS Interiors, volunteered her services. Ina never had the benefit of such a comforting room when she was 10 years old. Sarah wanted to change that for other children. She points out a box of Kleenex that is on the table. She says it's for the parents' tears.

Sarah and Arnie have also founded a scholarship in memory of Ina at the Corona Gym Club. The money goes toward a competitive team member who cannot afford the cost of being coached. As well, they have paid to equip an ambulance in Israel through the organization Magen David Adom for Israel. Sarah is on the board. The check for the ambulance was presented at the Saidye Bronfman Theatre in Montreal before the play, *Second Avenue.*

"Sarah and Arnie have certainly done their best to

honor Ina and to honor her memory," says family friend
Dr. Bill James, an Ottawa pediatrician. "That's very
important. They're taking their grief and helping others."
Dr. James also admires the level of commitment Sarah
and Arnie showed toward their children, and the way
they respected Ina's wishes when she was an adult. "Ina
did it her way," he says.

The Juvenile Diabetes Foundation has founded a
scholarship for researchers in Ina's name. The auxiliary of the seniors' home, Hillel Lodge, has donated a
state-of-the-art piano for its residents, as a tribute to
Ina. Sarah was president of the auxiliary for five years,
retiring from the job only recently. She loves spending time with elderly people, dancing the hora with
them, chatting with them, and taking them out to
lunch. One older woman once asked Sarah, "Why do
you bother with us?" and she answered, "From you,
I learn. You've lived life." Every year while she was
president, Sarah wrote a summary for the Vaad
report, an annual report for Jewish Community
Services. She never included a picture of herself, as is
usually done, but instead placed in the report a picture of one of the residents of Hillel Lodge or one of
her grandchildren. Her trademark quote for this
report was, "I know what it is like to be young. Do
you know what it is like to be old?"

The staff of the *Ottawa Business Journal* unveiled a
plaque honoring Ina, with a picture of her taken in their
offices. The *Ottawa Sun* also honored her by sponsoring
a scholarship for a journalism student at Carleton

University or Algonquin College. Ina's Hadassah chapter has named their group after Ina.

Harley, too, has done much to keep the memory of Ina alive, including designing a series of greeting cards. The outside of the cards depicts pictures of leaves and other symbols of the outdoors. On the inside are one of eight words—individuality, prosperity, equality, longevity, sensuality, tranquility, generosity and continuity. "We lost Ina to diabetes," the cards say. "Help find a cure." Proceeds go to the Juvenile Diabetes Foundation, and cards were on sale at three Artworks stores in Ottawa, which are owned by Arlie Koyman's family. Arlie, who recalls Ina spinning cartwheels along the street when the two were returning home from school and writing the *Puppy Press* and studying with Ina in the basement together, sometimes still picks up the phone to dial Ina, until she remembers.

Harley made a large charcoal drawing of Ina's face, which is now in Sarah and Arnie's home. He drew her eyebrows and eyes, her nose and her mouth. Her eyes sparkle. There's a dimple next to her mouth.

Harley and Jane speak about Ina to their children. Jared, on his sixth birthday, sent out a unique card to the children who were coming to his party. The message on the card was written by his parents, but the idea behind it came from Jared.

"A message from Jared. I have a special request. 2 years ago, my favorite aunt Ina passed away. Instead of your generous presents to celebrate my birthday, would you help me build a library of children's books for the sick kids at the Children's Hospital of Eastern Ontario? Each book will sit on a special bookshelf I am decorating. It'll be called Jared's library and will go in a playroom already in honor of Ina. Thank you for your help. (P.S. Don't worry—mom and dad have promised me lots of extra presents, so I won't be deprived!)"

Ina's death changed the way Arnie looks at life. "Things important before aren't important now. I get up. I do my stuff, but I don't have the same drive that I used to. I hold a lot of stuff in. I have my moments and I go off to my own little spot and I have my cry. It was something we didn't think was possible, to have her pass on. That was never in the picture, because we would never have allowed it."

When Ina's first cousin Heidi Lemish thinks about Ina, she smiles, she doesn't cry. "She was the brightest of the whole family. She was the happiest. She would ask, how can I help you? What can I do for you? She does deserve a book to be written. She does deserve scholarships in her name."

Sarah often wonders why Ina threw a surprise party for her on her 58th birthday. It took place soon before Ina was beeped for surgery. Usually the 58th birthday isn't celebrated in such a way. Did Ina think their time together was limited?

"Dear mom," Ina wrote in her birthday card for her mother.

Oh yah—SURPRISE! Just wanted to do some-

thing a little bit special for you after a few rough
years! Ya know we think you are the absolute greatest
mother, friend, bubbie, journalistic source and
grandma there is! We tease you lots but we really both
admire and respect you!
All our love,
Ina, Stuart, Joshua and Flash

"There is a word for a person who loses parents, and
that's an orphan. There's a word for someone who loses
a spouse, and that's a widow, or a widower. But there is
no word for a parent who loses a child."

Ina's funeral was crowded with so many people that
they overflowed into the hallway and listened to the ser-
vice through speakers. In all his years, Rabbi Bulka can
truthfully say he has never seen such a packed funeral at
the chapel.

It was Rabbi Bulka who coined the phrase "the Ina
way." In his remarks at Ina's funeral, Rabbi Bulka said,
"We are all in the state of shock; shocked at Ina's death,
shocked because she was doing so well, so well that she
was ready to resume her telephone connections with the
people she worked with. This was her mindset. At the
same time as we are shocked, if we look back at the ret-
rospect of Ina's life, we have to be amazed and over-
whelmed by her massive achievements in so short a
time, and in spite of all the obstacles that she faced. She
literally squeezed every ounce out of life that she could,
and that is no exaggeration. The message of her life is a
very clear one. That message is that you take in life what

is dealt to you and you try to make the very best of it. That is the way she lived. That was her life. Now we, without Ina, are faced with an enormous challenge, the challenge to live the way she did, but in her absence. I hope and pray that her enduring memory will inspire all of us, family and friends, to live life the Ina way, which is really the only way; to the full."